WHY ARE THEY SO POOR?

CAPITALISM:

A PEOPLE'S HISTORY

INTRODUCTION

If it is raining, then there are clouds. Rain doesn't come from nowhere. And an objective assessment shows, further, that the rain comes only from clouds. No imaginative "explanation" can make it come from some other source. And, in virtually the same way, if it is "raining" appalling world economic inequality and widespread poverty, and near constant war or threat of war in any number of countries across the globe, there are the "clouds" of global capitalism. These things don't come from nowhere, either. It is beyond dispute that capitalism runs the world, and has predominantly run it for about the last 245 years and, further, that it has shaped the world in its image. While we know elements of capitalism have been traced back almost to the Middle Ages, we place its effective beginning as the system we roughly recognize today at 1775, when the first Industrial Revolution was under way. The steam engine had been invented and improved and, along with the cotton gin, the power loom, new iron production processes, etc., was, by the early 1800's, having a trampoline effect on capitalism. This jump started manufacturing and the factory system, which was a catalyst for the banking and credit industry. And so on. Of course, emergent capitalism had already accumulated a great deal of capital from slavery and the slave trade, and would continue to do so, both in

Europe and in the U.S. This in itself stands as stunning testimony that it has no more of a conscience than does rain.

It's impossible to reasonably contend that the shocking conditions in the world are not the result of those 245 years of the economic rule of capitalism. Capitalism's track record *is* the record of those shocking conditions. One would think, given that monumental truth, we would hear the word spoken regularly. But the powers that be shudder to use or even acknowledge the word "capitalism" because they know that, among broad strata of the people, it has come to be the dirtiest word in our language. (The word came into wide use in the late 1800s.) It calls to mind too much of the ugly truth of what this deceitful and rapacious economic system has meant for the condition of the world and the vast majority of its people. It is almost never heard from the lips of presidents, congressmen, or TV news shows or commentators. Even during and since their corrupt 2008 "credit default-swap" global meltdown, the word "capitalism" was rarely spoken or written, not if it was meant to be heard or read by the broad population. And neither has it been broadly heard during the current pandemic. The political leaders and commentators are fond of using the terms "free market," "free trade," "free enterprise," and even "democracy" to label the ruling economic system, thereby hoping to lend it a sound of dignity and render it seemingly benign, and thereby hope to obscure its reality.

Of course, capitalism didn't invent suffering and exploitation, although it probably has set the world record for it. But if, or because, there was poverty, oppression, lack of medical care, and war, etc., during the system of feudalism/serfdom and monarchy in the 1600's, does that mean we hold those ruling structures of those times responsible for the horrors that are clearly prevalent today? Or are we supposed to insist that it's just the result of "human nature"? If we answer "yes" to either of those questions, we will get broad and enthusiastic applause from the powers that be, along with their great relief that our finger of guilt is not pointed at them and their political and economic system.

The argument by some, usually by those in the richer countries, that capitalism has *primarily* been good for the world, is patently false by even a casual survey of the destruction and deprivation left in its wake for at least two-thirds of humanity, and some say it's more like three-fourths. But the fact that a slice of humanity *has* benefited from capitalism is not just important but essential to its staying power for, without that slice, the system would have long ago been swept into the dustbin of history. The continued support by the satisfied majority of the populations in the top capitalist countries is the main factor in its social, political, and economic endurance.

As for the reasoning that, if capitalism spread spontaneously across the globe in the first place, doesn't that mean it must have been the "natural" instinct of humanity? No, it doesn't, because, for the most part, it didn't spread spontaneously. It was imposed. What spread spontaneously was ferocious opposition to it everywhere throughout Asia, Africa, and Latin America. Today, still, that imposition survives, due to overwhelming economic and military power.

Behind the foregoing is a veritable ocean of evidence. Capitalism indicts itself. We hope to give voice and context to some of that evidence, however briefly. Of course, it isn't I who presents the evidence. That's done by some of the many literary heroes who have already done it. Involved herein are many books, ranging in publishing dates from 1911 to 2017, each excerpted, some at length, which develop the history and thus help to illuminate the resulting current reality. These works are all highly recommended reading. Many articles and journals are also important, and generously used, particularly for describing the more recent economic relations and conditions.

Throughout this book, my comments (most of which occur in the second half) are either brief and in brackets ([ ]) within excerpts, or in type as is used in this *Introduction* when standing alone between excerpts.

D. N. Singerman, 2020

To Begin:

From an August 27, 1962 report in *Newsweek*:

Just a few hours by jet from New York or Chicago live more than 200 million people in the vast reaches of Latin America, and it is doubtful whether one-tenth of them know what it is like to go to bed with a full stomach. The great cities glitter opulently---Rio de Janeiro, Buenos Aires, Mexico City; but beneath the glitter and in the hinterland are odious and despondent slums where liquid-eyed Indian children scrounge for scraps and handouts while their parents labor for wages of twenty cents a day or less. This is the wasteland of the Western hemisphere, a land of misery whose poverty is as stark as any in the world.

In April, 1968, George W. Ball, U.S. diplomat, banker, and U.S. ambassador to the U.N., wrote:

[A]t least for the next several decades, the discontent of poorer nations does not threaten world destruction. Shameful as it undoubtedly may be, the world has lived at least two-thirds poor and one-third rich for generations. Unjust as it may be, the power of poor countries is limited.

THE "GREAT" PYRAMID---THE VIEW FROM THE BOTTOM

From *Inside the Third World*, Paul Harrison, 1984 (except where noted):

I remember the hunger of little boys in Kano, northern Nigeria---their sad faces covered in the white, flaky skin of kwashiorkor [malnutrition caused by lack of protein in the diet]. They had learned by heart the common West African beggar's plea, "Dash me money." I ate some cooked cassava for a snack and accidentally dropped a piece on the ground. Half a dozen of them leapt on it like a pack of wolves and fought each other desperately for it (276,277).

The distribution of the whole world's income is more unequal than even the most grotesquely unjust of national distributions. In 1976, the industrialized countries made up only 24 percent of the world's population, but raked in 78 percent of the income. The developing countries---76 percent of the people---got only 22 percent of the income. . . . The average developing country remained at around 7 percent of the average income of western countries. . . . Latin America, southern Asia, and Africa represented a smaller percentage of western incomes in 1975 than they did in 1950.

Two thirds seriously poor, two fifths destitute: these are the people who are gaining least, and often actually losing out, as their countries "develop." This immense army, legions of the damned in this life, is the bottom layer in the great international pyramid. They are the very crux of the development issue, for if development [and, indeed, progress itself] is to mean anything, it must mean the eradication of this great mass of suffering (pp. 405-406, 408-410).

[P]rivate property in land . . . is an extremely dangerous institution for the welfare of the poor. It leads to social polarization, increasing degrees of inequality, and grinding poverty among those without adequate access to land. . . . Almost everywhere in Asia it is the same story of commercial and technical progress, coupled with an increase in landlessness and poverty, and the death of the traditional systems that provided social security for everyone.

In rural Latin America . . . [t]he vast majority are landless laborers or owners of land so marginal that it cannot support a small family. . . . Landless laborers make up more than half the active population in Chile, Uruguay, Costa Rica and Argentina, and between 40 and 50 percent in Colombia, Mexico, Jamaica, and Nicaragua.

In Serra Pelada, Brazil, a small hamlet in the state of Rio Grande do Norte, the adobe and bamboo shacks of the workers straggle along the dirt road, penned outside the barbed wire around the big estates and their palatial ranch houses. In a rough field, a gang of six laborers is clearing weeds with their hoes. Every one of them is emaciated.

Like all the laborers of Serra Pelada, they have no land of their own. . . . Only at peak times can a laborer get a few weeks' solid work at a stretch---the rest of the year he may only get two or three days a week after endless treks around the ranches, cap in hand. . . . Because there is a large labor surplus, the landlords can always find takers to accept almost any wages or conditions they care to impose. And they themselves make sure there is a labor surplus, by keeping vast stretches of land abandoned under weeds and shrubs. . . . [P]eople are dying of malnutrition and its effects while good land lays waste next to their homes. . . . [I]n the seven countries it surveyed, the Inter-American Commission for Agricultural Development found that, on average, five out of every six hectares of estate land were unused.

In central Java, in Indonesia, almost every able-bodied man spends several months of the year away from home. . . . Everyone here is poor, everyone is on the lookout for extra work. Supar Kristanto owns only five hundred square meters of land, no more than a garden around his house. There is no hope of regular employment as an agricultural laborer in the area, so he is forced to go to Jakarta, selling cooked food from a little stall. He comes back once a month, bringing back about five thousand rupiahs ($12) each time. Rajilk, a twenty-five-year-old with one child, owns half a hectare: but you need about a hectare and a half in this area to be self-sufficient. Four times a year he goes to the regional capital . . . for two or three weeks at a time. There he joins the throng of cycle rickshaw drivers who line every street. Competition is so stiff that he is lucky if he earns 500 rupiahs ($1.20) in a day. He spends his nights sleeping on the three-foot-long seat, legs up: it saves money and protects the rickshaw against thieves.

In India, the building sites of Bombay or Calcutta are full of seasonal laborers. They live in ragged tented camps like the hordes of Genghis Khan. The landless laborers of Rajasthan move to Delhi or Ahmadabad for the dry season, when there is no work to be had on the land---and their women and children go, too (108-111, 113, 140).

National boundaries are no deterrent to the determined migrant. A steady stream of workers, most of them from rural areas, flows north and west from the Third World into the rich First World. In the 1960's, the UN-affiliated International Labor Office estimates, 5.1 million migrants from poor countries joined this long trek for work. In 1980, some estimates put their number as high as 20 million (141).

The United Nations Food and Agriculture Organization estimated that in the early 1970s there were 455 million people in the Third World getting less than the minimum intake of food required to keep body and soul together in the long term.

The total food resources available in the world would be perfectly adequate to feed everyone properly if they were fairly distributed among nations and social groups. . . . Much of the best land that should be used for domestic food production in the developing countries is growing cash crops for the West: five of the most common [are] sugar, tobacco, coffee, cocoa, and tea. In north-east Brazil, dense stands of thick green sugar cane wave their silvery tassels in the breeze, while the laborers who plant and cut it are squeezed onto the roadsides in their little huts. . . . [I]n Latin America, cattle are being raised on prime agricultural land for export to the West or consumption by local elites.

And, the incidence of illness in the poor countries is on a scale quite unimaginable to the incubated westerner. Threadworms infest one billion people, trachoma and hookworms afflict half a billion each. . . . Infant mortality takes a terrible toll. . . . In the poorest districts a baby may have little better than a sixty-forty chance of survival. . . . [P]arents have learned to live with infant mortality and accept child illness and death stoically; it is one of the tragedies of their lives.

Illness in general can be looked on as a kind of disease that thrives in the environment of poverty and perpetuates it. Behind almost every tropical disease life-cycle lies a set of social and physical conditions which are, for the most part, not adopted out of choice, but out of poverty. Simply wearing shoes, for example, would prevent parasites like bilharzia or hookworm from penetrating the feet. People in the Third World do not go barefoot out of ignorance or for cultural reasons---shoes are now seen as desirable everywhere, and people wear them without much thought for their health benefits. If the poor do not wear shoes, it is for one reason only: they cannot afford them, often enough for themselves, but certainly not for the growing feet of their children. Poor nutrition contributes to disease, but no one eats badly out of choice. It is not from ignorance of nutritional principles that the Sri Lanka tea laborer lives on unleavened bread, the Brazilian sugar worker on tortillas or the Javanese smallholder on plain rice (282-283,287,289-290).

The suffering and poverty of the Sri Lankan tea workers was typical of the tribulations imposed on the poor of the Third World by their countries' place in the international economic order. . . . The dwelling of Puryana Supaya, a thirty-seven-year-old Tamil . . . was typical of those I saw: a dark cell about ten feet square without windows that had to serve as bedroom, kitchen and living room for Supaya, his wife, and their three young children. It was in a row of about twenty similar dwellings back to back with another row. Supaya's cell was bare of all possessions except two cooking pots. The Supayas were lucky if they averaged more than 200 rupees (about $26) a month between them. They can afford nothing but food, though they never eat meat or fish. I asked Supaya what they ate that day. He showed me a plain, flat chapatti bread: they had three of those each, and that was all. The misery of people like Supaya was paying for the western housewife's cheap cup of tea (333-335).

The private property system molds the production system: 1.5 percent of the agricultural landlords own half of all the cultivable land, and every year Latin America spends more than $500 million on importing food that its own broad and fertile lands could produce without difficulty. Hardly 5 percent of the total area is under cultivation: the lowest proportion---and consequently the greatest waste---on earth. . . . The oligarchy and technocracy have tirelessly elaborated projects [of agrarian reform]. Dozens of projects---fat ones, thin ones, broad and narrow ones---gather dust on the shelves of every Latin American parliament. No curse is attached anymore to the theme of agrarian reform: politicians have learned that the best way not to have it is to keep invoking it (*Open Veins*, 126-128).

Poverty and inequality in developing nations are often described as if they were almost a natural phenomenon. Or as if they were the unintended outcome of unfortunate mistakes. Or as an inevitable, if regrettable and temporary, necessity on the runway towards economic take-off. In reality, gross inequality is rarely an accident. It is more usually the result of deliberate and calculated attempts by the rich to increase their wealth. . . . Often this can be done only at the cost of greater absolute poverty.

It is wealth that helps western interests to be well organized: governments have large reserves, manufacturers can afford to hold stocks off the market to keep prices up, workers have strike funds, social security, and unemployment pay. Conversely, Third World governments are poorly organized because they are poor. They often have to go on producing, even at low prices, because they have low reserves and need the money to stay solvent. They do not control the marketing of their produce: the companies of London, New York, and Tokyo do it for them (except in the case of oil). . . . [S]mall farmers cannot afford to stop producing, or build up stockpiles, if prices fall. They are poor enough to need whatever money they can get just to survive (331, 333-335, 337-340, 345).

Much of the [foreign] multinational corporations' income comes from charges for intellectual property. . . . [They] keep a tight grip on their knowhow. One study of five countries (India, Turkey, Egypt, Pakistan, and Trinidad) found that 89 percent of all patents were owned by foreigners. In Chile the proportion of foreign-owned patents rose from 65 percent in 1937 to 95 percent in 1967. . . . And the technology supplied was rarely offered without restrictive conditions attached. The technological dependence of developing countries arises in part from the massive concentration of scientists and research in the West. . . . The West, with its higher salary levels, drained off around 30,000 of these [from the underdeveloped countries] every year over the 1960's. Between the early years of that decade and 1972, the United States acquired 90,000 Third World brains, the United Kingdom gained 84,000 and Canada 56,000. The United Nations Conference on Trade and Development has calculated that this human traffic . . . was worth a total of $51 billion to these three countries alone (348-351).

[And] the much publicized advances of the whiz-kids [3rd World economic "stars"] will not alter the fundamental problems of underdevelopment.

India, which was already in 1976 the thirteenth largest economic power in the world, has the third biggest urban population, and has more trained scientists than most

European countries. Her immense industrial capacity covers a wide range of products and she is now becoming a large exporter of both manufactures and of machinery. Yet her per capita income in 1976 was only $150, one of the poorest in the world. Outside the cities and a few privileged states, the poverty of the 80 percent who live in India's villages is so massive in its inertia that it has scarcely been budged by the bustling expansion of the modern sector.

[Or] take the example of Brazil, whose former president, Emilio Medici, aptly remarked that the country was doing well but its inhabitants were not. Brazil's 1976 gross national product makes her the tenth biggest economic power in the world . . . but, overall, perhaps half the people of Brazil still suffer from acute poverty, overcrowding, disease, malnutrition, unemployment, and official neglect (429-431).

Robert McNamara, the World Bank president [1968-1981] who was chairman of Ford Motor Co. and then Secretary of Defense, [announced that] the World Bank will give priority in its loans to [3rd World] countries that implement birth control plans. The United States is more concerned than any other country with spreading and imposing "family planning" in the farthest outposts. Not only the government, but the Rockefeller and the Ford foundations as well, have nightmares about millions of children advancing like locusts over the horizon from the third world. . . . Various U.S. missions have sterilized thousands of women in Amazonia, although this is the least populated habitable zone on our planet. Most Latin American countries have no real surplus of people; on the contrary, they have too few. Brazil has thirty-eight times fewer inhabitants per square mile than Belgium, Paraguay has forty-nine times fewer than England, Peru has thirty-two times fewer than Japan. Haiti and El Salvador, the human ant-heaps of Latin America, have lower population densities than Italy. [This over-population pretext] to justify the very unequal income distribution between countries and social classes . . . is an insult to the intelligence. And the real intentions anger us (*Open Veins*, 2, 5-6, 8).

[T]he shocking fact [is] that in 1984, there were more absolutely poor people in the world than in 1960. There were more unemployed and under-employed, more children out of school, more illiterate adults, more people without clean water and sanitation, and more malnourished people. . . . This . . . can only be read as progress if one abstracts from the human realities (464-465).

THE CURSE OF "MONOCULTURE"

From *Open Veins of Latin America*, Eduardo Galeano, 1971:

Sugar had destroyed Brazil's Northeast. The humid coastal fringe, well watered by rains, has a soil of great fertility, rich in humus and mineral salts, and covered by forests. This region of tropical forests was turned into a region of savannas. Naturally fitted to produce food, it became a place of hunger. Where everything had bloomed exuberantly, the destructive and all-dominating latifundio [large, privately owned, commercial landed estates, usually raising cash crops for export] left sterile rock, washed-out soil, and eroded lands. At first there had been orange and mango plantations, but these were left to their fate, or reduced to small orchards surrounding the sugarmill owner's house. . . . Fire was used to clear land for cane fields, devastating the fauna along with the flora: deer, wild boar, tapir, rabbit, pacas, and armadillo disappeared. All was sacrificed on the altar of sugarcane monoculture. In the city of Recife in the Northeast, a third of the population lives in miserable hovels; in one district, more than half the babies die before they are a year old (62, 64, 72, 77-78).

And some people rank coffee almost on a par with oil in its importance on the international market. . . . [W]ith Brazil's abolition of slavery in 1888, an army of free farmhands would accompany coffee on its travels. The Rio Paraiba became the country's richest area, to be quickly ruined by a plant whose destructive form of cultivation left forests razed, natural reserves exhausted, and general decadence in its wake. Previously virgin lands were pitilessly eroded as the plunder-march of coffee advanced.

Coffee is also basic to the economy of El Salvador [and Haiti]: monoculture [an economy forced to rely largely on the export of one crop or other raw material] makes it necessary to import the beans [as well as] the people's only source of protein---corn, vegetables, and other foods the country had traditionally produced. A quarter of all Salvadorans die of . . . severe vitamin deficiency. As for Haiti, it has Latin America's highest death rate, and more than half of its children are anemic. The wages Haiti requires by law belong in the department of science fiction: actual wages on coffee plantations vary from $.07 to $.15 a day.

In Colombia, also, coffee is king. According to a Time magazine report in 1962, only 5 percent of the price yielded by coffee in its journey from tree to U.S. consumer goes into the wages of the workers who produce it. . . . The price breakdown is as follows: 40 percent for middlemen, exporters, and importers; 10 percent for taxes imposed by both governments; 10 percent for transport; 5 percent for publicity by the Pan-American Coffee Bureau; 30 percent for plantation owners; and 5 percent for workers' wages.

In the United States and Europe, coffee creates income and jobs and mobilizes substantial capital; in Latin America it pays hunger wages and sharpens economic deformation. It provides work for more than 600,000 people in the United States: those who distribute and sell Latin American coffee there earn infinitely more than the Brazilians, Colombians, Guatemalans, Salvadorans, and Haitians who plant and harvest it on the plantations. . . . [The 3rd World "participates" in global capitalism the same way that the victim, with puncture marks on its neck, participates in vampire-ism.]

[T]he United Nations published [in the mid-1950's] the results of a study of nutrition in Colombia: 88 percent of

Bogota [the capital city] schoolchildren suffered from avitaminosis, 78 percent from riboflavinosis, and more than half were below normal weight; avitaminosis affected 71 percent of workers and 78 percent of Tensa Valley peasants. The study showed "a marked insufficiency of protective foods---milk and its derivatives, eggs, meat, fish, and some fruits and vegetables---which together provide protein, vitamins, and salt." It is not only the flash of gunfire that reveals social tragedy. . . . Coffee locked the region firmly into the world market (92, 94-102, 104-105).

In the middle of the 19th century, with Europe's population climbing steeply, it was urgently necessary to revive exhausted soil so that food production could grow in the same proportion. The value of guano as fertilizer was demonstrated in British laboratories, and after 1840 it began to be exported from Peru on a large scale. Since time immemorial pelicans and seagulls, feeding on the prodigious shoals of fish in the coastal currents, had been accumulating mountains of excrement rich in nitrogen, ammonia, phosphates, and alkaline salts: on these rainless shores the guano had remained in a pure state. . . . [B]y 1850, it was being used intensively to fertilize European fields. Thanks to the sodium nitrate and the guano lying on Pacific coasts, almost within reach of the ships that came to fetch them, the specter of hunger departed from Europe.

[T]he desert had served as a damper on latent conflicts between Chile, Peru, and Bolivia, but now nitrates brought them to the boil. The War of the Pacific broke out in 1879 and lasted until 1883. Chile's armed forces, having occupied the Peruvian nitrate ports, finally entered Lima [Peru] as conquerors. By 1890, more than half of Chile's income came from the export of nitrates. In the same period, British investments in Chile more than tripled: the nitrate region became a British factory. . . . Meanwhile, Chileans put in sixteen-hour workdays without even Sundays off, and were paid in scrip that lost about half its value at the company stores.

Between 1886 and 1890, the Chilean state under President Jose Manuel Balmaceda undertook the most ambitious development plan in its history. . . . [Among other things], he announced that the nitrate areas must be nationalized through the formation of Chilean enterprises, and refused to sell state-owned nitrate fields to the British. Three years later civil war broke out. [A handful of British nitrate capitalists] generously financed the rebels and British warships blockaded the Chilean coast while the London press fulminated against Balmaceda, a "butcher" and "dictator of the worst stripe." Balmaceda was defeated, and killed himself. The British ambassador informed the Foreign Office: "The British community makes no secret of its satisfaction over the fall of Balmaceda, whose victory, it is thought, would have implied serious harm to British commercial interests."

On the eve of World War I, two-thirds of Chile's national income came from nitrate exports, but it was a prosperity which, far from developing and diversifying, only heightened the country's . . . deformations. Chile functioned as an appendage of the British economy. And then a German chemist, sitting in his laboratory, [perfected] the Haber process, which produces nitrates by fixing nitrogen from the air, decisively displacing Chilean nitrate and sending Chile's economy into a tailspin. . . .

Peru . . . retained [after the 1879-83 War of the Pacific] guano deposits on the northern coast. Guano remained the chief fertilizer for Peruvian agriculture, until the fish meal boom wiped out the pelicans and seagulls after 1960. The fishing concerns, mostly from the United States, quickly destroyed the anchovy shoals near the coast to feed U.S. and European pigs and poultry with Peruvian fishmeal, and the guano-producing birds took off after the fishing boats, ever further out to sea. Without the strength to fly back, they fell in the ocean. Others stayed put, so that in 1962 and 1963 one could see flocks of pelicans hunting for food along Lima's main avenue; when they could no longer take wing, they died on the streets (139-143).

And from *How Europe Underdeveloped Africa*, Walter Rodney, 1972. [Walter Rodney, from Guyana, was an internationally acclaimed author, historian, and social and political activist in pursuit of African self-determination and advancement. In June of 1980, he was killed by a bomb placed in his car.]:

In recent times, economists have been recognizing in colonial and post-colonial Africa a pattern that has been termed "growth without development." That phrase has now appeared as the title of books on Liberia and Ivory Coast. It means that goods and services of a certain type are on the increase. There may be more rubber and coffee exported, there may be more cars imported with the proceeds, and there may be more gasoline stations built to service the cars. But the profit goes abroad, and the economy becomes more and more a dependency of the metropoles. In no African colony was there economic integration [inter-connected branches of economic development], or any provision for making the economy self-sustained and geared to its own local goals. Therefore, there was growth of the . . . import-export sector, but the only things which developed were dependency and underdevelopment.

A further revelation of growth without development under colonialism is [as was previously noted as well in the countries of Latin America) the overdependence on one or two exports. The term "monoculture" is used to describe those colonial economies which were centered around a single crop. Liberia . . . was a monoculture dependent on rubber, Gold Coast on cocoa, Dahomey and southeast Nigeria on palm produce, Sudan and Uganda on cotton, Tanganyika on sisal. In Senegal and Gambia, groundnuts accounted for 85 to 90 per cent of money earnings. In effect, two African colonies were told to grow nothing but peanuts.

Every farming people has a staple food, plus a variety of other supplements. Historians, agronomists, and botanists have all contributed to showing the great variety of such foods within the pre-colonial African economy. There were numerous crops which were domesticated within the African continent, there were several wild food species . . . and Africans had shown no conservatism in adopting useful food plants of Asian or American origin. Diversified agriculture was within the African tradition. Monoculture was a colonialist invention.

Sometimes, cash crops were grown to the exclusion of staple foods---thus causing famines. For instance, in Gambia rice farming was popular before the colonial era, but so much of the best land was transferred to groundnuts that rice had to be imported on a large scale to try to counter the fact that famine was becoming endemic. . . . [And] when the [cash] crop was affected by internal factors such as disease, it amounted to an overwhelming disaster, as in the case of Gold Coast cocoa when it was hit by swollen-shoot disease in the 1940s. Besides, at all times, the price fluctuations (which were [and are] externally controlled) left the African producer helpless. From a capitalist viewpoint, monocultures commended themselves most because they made colonial economies entirely dependent on the metropolitan buyers of their produce (234-235).

[A]ttention must be drawn to one of the most important consequences of colonialism on African development, and that is the stunting effect on Africans as a physical species. Colonialism created conditions which led not just to periodic famine but to chronic undernourishment, malnutrition, and deterioration in the physique of the African people. If such a statement sounds wildly extravagant, it is only because propaganda has conditioned even Africans to believe that malnutrition and starvation were the *natural* lot of Africans from time immemorial. . . . [I]t is useful to point to those African peoples who until today have managed to maintain their own pattern of existence insofar as food is concerned. The pastoral Masai, Galla, Ankoli, Batutsi, and Somali are all in that category. Their physique is generally so superb, their resistance and endurance so great, that they have become the objects of scientific research.

Investigators who have studied the nutritional conditions of "primitive" Africans in tropical Africa are unanimous in stating that they show no clinical signs of dietary deficiency. One of the most striking indications of the superiority of the indigenous African diet is the magnificent condition of the teeth. One researcher working among six ethnic groups in Kenya could not find a single case of tooth decay, not a single deformation of dental arch. But when those same people were transplanted and put on the "civilized" diet available under colonialism, their teeth began to decay at once (236-238).

Lizzie Collingham describes in her book, *The Taste of Empire*, the results of a nutrition study of the Kikuyu people of Kenya conducted between 1927 and 1929 and published in 1931. Collingham says of that report:

One positive consequence of the Kenyan nutritional study was that it brought the problem of malnutrition in the colonies to light and led to the setting up in 1936 of a Committee on Nutrition in the Colonial Empire. The committee commissioned reports on the nutritional health of the colonies and the findings were damning. Jamaica, Antigua, West Africa, the Far East, Mauritius, and Ceylon [now Sri Lanka] all returned evidence that malnutrition was an Empire-wide problem. . . . The governors of Jamaica and Antigua concluded that poverty was the cause of underfeeding. "Parents cannot afford to buy food," stated the senior medical officer on Antigua. On the Gold Coast the director of the medical department identified the attention devoted to mining and cocoa as detrimental to subsistence farming and forest conservation. Besides poverty, low wages, poor yields and the lack of food crops, the ignorance of "Government officials and those who have power over the nutrition of others" was identified as one of the primary causes of malnutrition (*Taste of Empire*, 246-47).

AMERICAN "EXCEPTIONALISM"

From *Open Veins of Latin America* (except where noted):

[In Brazil], the rise of coffee as a new "king product" produced the 1850 Law of Lands which denied ownership of land to those who worked it when the great spaces of the interior . . . were being opened up. This law was subsequently reinforced and ratified . . . by abundant legislation that decreed purchase as the only form of access to land. . . . U.S. legislation in the same period had the opposite aim: it was to promote the internal colonization of the country. Covered wagons rolled westward into virgin lands with pioneers who extended the frontier at the cost of slaughtered Indians. The Homestead Act of 1862 assured every family of ownership of a quarter section, a lot one-half mile square; each beneficiary committed himself to farm his parcel for a minimum of five years. The public domain was colonized with startling speed and the population grew and spread like a great oil smear. The fertile land that was to be had almost gratis drew European peasants like a magnet: they crossed the ocean and then the Appalachians onto the wide-open prairies. As the country grew in extent and population, unemployment was avoided by the creation of farm jobs, and at the same time an internal market---the multitude of farmer-proprietors---was generated with substantial purchasing power to sustain industrial development.

In contrast, the rural workers who have pushed Brazil's frontier inland for more than a century have been . . . braceros contracted to serve latifundistas who have already taken possession of the great open spaces. . . . These two opposite systems of internal colonization reveal one of the most important differences between U.S. and Latin American development models. . . . New England colonists, the original nucleus of U.S. civilization, never acted as colonial agents for European capitalist accumulation: their own development, and the development of their new land, was always their motivation. The thirteen colonies served as an outlet for the army of European peasants and artisans who were being thrown off the labor market by metropolitan development. . . . [I]nternal economic development was never the goal of the ruling classes of Latin American colonial society. Their profits came from outside; they were tied more to the foreign market than to their own domain. . . . Goods moved along the roads in only one direction: to the port and overseas markets. This also provides the key to the United States' expansion as a national unit and to the fragmentation of Latin America. Our production centers are not interconnected but take the form of a fan with a far-away vertex.

[Furthermore], one might say that the thirteen colonies . . . show the great importance of not being born important. For the north of America had no gold or silver, no Indian civilizations with dense concentrations of people already organized for work, no fabulously fertile tropical soil on the coastal fringe. . . . Those colonists were lucky. Furthermore, the northern colonies, from Maryland to New England to Nova Scotia, had a climate and soil similar to British agriculture and produced exactly the same things. The situation in the Antilles [Islands] and the mainland [South America] Spanish-Portuguese colonies was quite different. Tropical lands produced sugar, tobacco, cotton, indigo, turpentine; a small Caribbean island had more economic importance for England than the thirteen colonies that would become the United States.

The truth is that the economic insignificance of the thirteen colonies permitted the early diversification of their exports and set off the early and rapid development of manufacturing. Even before independence, North American industrialization had official encouragement and protection. England took a tolerant attitude while it strictly forbade its Antillean islands to manufacture so much as a pin (130-133).

But Britain was eager to get iron from its colonies. Maryland made it governmental policy to encourage iron furnaces as of 1719, and the Chesapeake became a leader in colonial iron production. These ironworks produced only bars, or "pigs," because as codified in the Iron Act of 1750 the colonists were not to have rolling, plating, or slitting mills, much less to make steel of their own. The colonials were to be consumers, not manufacturers, so they weren't allowed even to work iron into the rods used in the manufacture of nails, because supplying nails to plantations was a British business. Americans were expected to buy their iron back in the form of finished nails from the West Midlands naileries, with the cost of two ocean voyages factored into the price. [While the Iron Act demonstrates Britain's and other European powers' general colonial policy, carried out with a vengeance throughout the Caribbean and southern hemisphere, it apparently was largely disregarded in the North American colonies] (*The American Slave Coast*, 201).

In 1631, the recently arrived colonists in Boston launched a thirty-ton sloop, Blessing of the Bay . . . and from then on the shipping industry grew rapidly. Massachusetts subsidized production of hemp for rigging and ropes, and also encouraged local manufacture of canvas and sails. To the north and south of Boston the coasts were dotted with prosperous shipyards. The colonial governments extended subsidies and premiums to all kinds of manufacture. There were incentives to promote the production of flax and wool, raw materials for crude fabrics. To exploit Lynn iron deposits, the first foundry went into operation in 1643; soon Massachusetts was supplying iron to the whole region. . . . England paid such scant attention to these colonies in the eighteenth century that they were able to introduce the latest metropolitan techniques into their factories, turning restrictive colonial pacts into scraps of paper. This was far from true of the Latin American colonies (*Open Veins*, 201,202).

THE WEAPONS OF "FREE" TRADE & "FREE" MARKETS

From *OPEN VEINS* (except where noted):

In 1812, British traders were reporting to the Foreign Office that, in Argentina, they had succeeded in replacing German and French textiles; and they had also replaced Argentine textile production, which was strangled by the "free-trade" port. The same occurred with variations elsewhere in Latin America.

From Yorkshire, Lancashire, the Cheviot Hills, and Wales poured an endless stream of cotton and woolens, iron and leather, wood and porcelain goods. Manchester's looms, Sheffield's foundries, Worcester and Staffordshire potteries flooded Latin American markets. Free trade enriched the ports which lived from exports, lifted sky-high the extravagance of oligarchies determined to enjoy every known luxury, but ruined budding local manufacture and frustrated expansion of the internal market. . . . Latin American manufactures continued fitfully, with one foot in the grave and with no possibility of sustained long-term development.

In Chile, one of Spain's most far-flung possessions, isolation at first favored the development of industrial activity from the beginnings of colonial life. It had spinning mills, textile mills, and tanneries; all the ships of the South Seas were equipped with Chilean rigging and cordage; it manufactured metal objects, from retorts and guns to ornaments, fine tableware, and clocks, and built boats and vehicles. But, like Brazil's textile and metal works, which took their modest first steps in the eighteenth century, they were wiped out by foreign imports. . . . Latin America's big ports, through which the wealth of its soil and subsoil passed en route to distant centers of power, were being built up as instruments of the conquest and domination of the countries to which they belonged, and as conduits through which to drain the nations' income. While ports and capitals strove to be like Paris or London, behind them stretched the desert. . . . In the twentieth century . . . peasants flee from their villages in the mountains and on the plains and flood into Buenos Aires to offer their labor: like the peasants of other poor provinces, they get no further than the city's outskirts, where they settle down beside 700,000 other inhabitants of the "villas miserias" and make out as best they can with crumbs from the great capital's banquet table (175-179, 187).

Free trade involved a frenzied increase in imports, especially of luxury articles; governments contracted debts, which in turn called for new loans, so that a minority could live fashionably. . . . [T]he process was similar throughout Latin America---and still is, although the creditors, and some of the mechanisms, have changed. . . . These republics' histories may be said to be that of the economic obligations they incur to the all-absorbing world of European finance. . . . Buenos Aires province had been completely mortgaged---all its revenues, all its public lands---as guarantee of payment. As the finance minister in the period when the loan was contracted [1824] said: "We are not in a position to take measures against foreign trade, particularly British, because we are bound to that nation by large debts and would expose ourselves to a rupture which would cause much harm. . . ." By the middle of the nineteenth century, servicing of the foreign debt absorbed almost 40 percent of Brazil's budget, and every country was caught in the same trap (198-199).

Latin America's external debt in 1975 was almost three times greater than it was in 1969. In 1975 approximately half of Brazil's, Mexico's, Chile's, and Uruguay's incomes from exports went for amortization and interest on the debt, and for paying the profits of foreign concerns operating in those countries. Servicing of debt and profit remittances in that year swallowed 55 percent of Panama's exports and 60 percent of Peru's (276-277).

"There are two ways of conquering a foreign nation. One is to gain control of its people by force of arms; the other is to gain control of its economy by financial means."--- Secretary of State [1953-1959] John Foster Dulles (*The Enemy*, 153).

Railroads formed another decisive part of the cage of dependency. . . . Many of the loans were for financing railroads to bring minerals and foodstuffs to export terminals. The tracks were laid not to connect internal areas one with another, but to connect production centers with ports. The design still resembles the fingers of an open hand: thus railroads, so often hailed as forerunners of progress, were an impediment to the formation and development of an internal market. . . . [F]reightage on articles [refined] in the Argentine interior was much higher than on unfinished goods. Railroad charges became a curse that made it impossible to manufacture cigarettes in tobacco-growing areas, to spin and weave in wool centers, or to finish wood in forest zones. When the railroads were booming, the British concerns had often obtained considerable land concessions on either side of the tracks, in addition to the railbeds themselves. A fabulous gift to the Brazilian railway in 1911 led to the burning of countless huts and the eviction or death of peasant families in the concession area. It was this that triggered off the "Contestado" revolt, one of the greatest outbursts of popular fury in Brazilian history (199-200).

Fortune, in 1967, assessed the "enticing new opportunities" which the Latin American Common Market [LACM] opens to northern business: "In many a boardroom, the common market is becoming a serious element in planning for the future. . . . The magazine cited examples of "rationalizing" or "expanding" operations by corporations such as ITT, General Electric, Remington Rand, Otis Elevator, Worthington, Firestone, Deere, Westinghouse, Air Brake, and American Machine and Foundry. Nine years ago [1962] Raul Prebisch, a vigorous advocate of a Latin American common market and free trade, wrote: "Another argument I often hear, from Mexico to Buenos Aires, is that the Common Market will offer foreign industry opportunities for expansion that it does not now have in our limited markets. . . . It is feared that the benefits offered by the Common Market will be taken advantage of principally by foreign industry, and not by national industries. . . . I shared and share this fear, not only in imagination but because I have verified the reality of that fact in practice.". . .

[In fact], [t]he Central American Common Market, an effort to join the deformed economies of five countries, has served to blow down with one puff the national producers of cloth, paint, medicines, cosmetics, and biscuits, and to expand the profits and trading orbit of [many major U.S. corporations] (254-256).

And from *Empire of Cotton, a Global History,* Sven Beckert, 2014:

In large parts of Africa, observed Thomas Ellison as late as 1886, "indigenous cotton has from time immemorial been both grown and manufactured, and the natives are for the most part clothed in fabrics of their own production." . . . Yet, while local and regional networks persisted, they would never again flourish. These smaller networks . . . were undermined by the ever-widening veins of European capital and its state power.

Tench Coxe [American political economist] understood that process already in 1818: the export of British piece goods to India, he perceptively observed, would force Indians "to turn to raising cotton instead of making piece goods they cannot sell" [because of the flood of cheaper British goods---commodities, one might say, consciously deployed, not only for profit, but as weapons of destruction and coercion].

Pushed by Lancashire manufacturers and cotton merchants from Liverpool to Bombay, the British colonial government in India continued its project, which had accelerated significantly during the U.S. Civil War [when the availability of raw cotton was sorely restricted], of promoting the transformation of the cotton-growing countryside. The impact was swift: in India as late as 1853, Berar had remained largely removed from world markets, with a village-oriented economy with a substantial household manufacturing sector. By the 1870s, however, much of Berar's economic activity focused on the production of raw cotton for world markets. A British colonial official observed by the middle of that decade that in Berar, "Cotton is grown almost entirely for export. The manufacture of home cloth has been undermined by the importation of English Piece Goods, and many of the weaver class have become ordinary laborers."

Indeed, forty years later a gazetteer could report that Berar's once thriving cotton manufacturing industry had all but disappeared "since the advent of the railway." As Rivett-Carnac [chairman of the British East India Company] explained in 1869:

"Now it is not too much to hope that, with a branch railway to this tract, European piece goods might be imported so as to undersell the native cloth. And the effect would be that, not only would a larger supply of the raw material be obtained . . . but the large population now employed in spinning and weaving would be made available for agricultural labor, and thus the jungle land might be broken up and the cultivation extended."

[As] British Secretary of State for India, Charles Wood, [stated], "The conclusions drawn from the Cotton papers are on the whole satisfactory. The Native weavers are exactly the class of people whom I remember in my early days on the Moor Edges in the West Riding [rural northern England]. Every small farmer had 20 to 50 acres of land and two or three looms in his house. The factories and mills destroyed all weaving of this kind and now they are exclusively agriculturalists. Your Indian hybrids [people who combined farming and household manufacturing] will end in the same way." Contemporaries like Wood understood that they were part of a grand move to transform the world's countryside into the producer of raw materials and consumer of [British] manufactured goods [as well as, eventually, a supplier of labor to factories], and they took pride in their role.

A . . . growing number of rural cultivators turned into poorly paid wage workers in the world's cotton fields. They were the least powerful. Often their descent into wage work had been the result of their worsening situation as highly indebted sharecroppers, tenants, or owners of small farms. Becoming a wage worker was a measure of their defeat. In Egypt, by 1907, nearly 40 percent of all agriculturalists had become landless laborers. In India as well, the number of wage workers on cotton lands tended to increase across the nineteenth century. . . . [T]he greater orientation toward cotton agriculture . . . resulted in an ever-increasing percentage of land devoted to the white gold. . . . In northern Mexico, too, [wage-labor] swept the cotton fields. After 1884, landowners in La Laguna made use of new railroads and a new irrigation infrastructure to build a huge cotton-growing complex, making it Mexico's most important commercial agricultural area. Tens of thousands of workers populated the fields . . . as the rural population, many of them migrants from elsewhere in Mexico, increased from twenty thousand to two hundred thousand between 1880 and 1910, with an additional forty thousand migrant workers arriving during harvest time. As a result, the cotton farms expanded at breakneck speed. . . . Many of these workers eventually arrived in La Laguna on private rail lines, packed like cattle in boxcars. Since there was no land available for these migrants, there was no possibility of engaging in subsistence agriculture. . . . [C]reating markets for metropolitan manufacturers was a conscious project of colonial administrations. The global South was to be a market for metropolitan industry, not a competitor, and a supplier of raw materials and labor, and both required the destruction of indigenous manufacturing.

Despite individual resistance and collective protest, the overall trend was unwavering and ultimately devastating: . . . In India alone, historian Tirthankar Roy concluded, "There is undeniable empirical evidence that the community of hand-spinners gave up spinning on a large scale, and this factor alone may account for a loss of industrial employment to the extent of 4-5 million persons." Other historians have suggested that the loss of manufacturing between 1830 and 1860 amounted to between 2 and 6 million full-time jobs just in India. . . .

Yet, most crucially, the radical recasting of ever larger swaths of the world's countryside . . . undermined food security. During the American Civil War [as one stark example], British officials . . . reported that [in Third World colonies] "the increasing area of land devoted to cultivation of Articles of Export, such as Cotton . . . [has led to a] proportionate decrease in cultivation of articles of food." As a result, food prices rose between 1861 and 1865 by more than 325 percent, and even Sir Charles Trevelyan had to admit that "at the present high prices of food, the body of the people, in several parts of India, is barely able to subsist." In Egypt, the situation was quite similar. Once a grain-exporting country, it became dependent on imports of food crops as the result of its greater dedication to cotton during the American Civil War. When in the summer of 1863 disease killed nearly all of Egypt's cattle, a food crisis emerged in which tens of thousands of *felaheen* [agricultural laborers] perished.

The increasing world market orientation of cotton cultivators also had significant effects on social structures. Throughout western India's Maharashtra, for example, British efforts to increase revenue and encourage peasants to participate in distant markets led to the undermining of the collective nature of villages, making individual peasants instead of villages as a whole responsible for taxes, and handing judicial power to distant courts instead of village-based and peasant-dominated tribunals. The market now increasingly subsumed all aspects of society, not just in Lancashire or Alsace, but Berar and Lower Egypt as well. In Egypt, the booming cotton export industry, according to historian Alan Richards, "destroyed the old quasi-communal forms of land tenure, broke up the protective web of village social relations, replaced them with private property in land and individual tax responsibility, and helped create four classes: large landowners . . . rich peasants . . . small peasant landowners, and a landless class." As early as the 1840s, the government had begun compelling peasants to grow specific crops, including cotton, and to "deliver them to government warehouses." Peasants had responded to this pressure by leaving the land in droves, which the government took as a reason to deny any claims to the land by those who had "deserted" it. By 1862, anyone who left the land for more than two months lost his claim to the property. . . .

The most serious impact on cotton farmers, however, emerged after the American Civil War. . . . [W]orld market integration increased the economic uncertainty faced by people in remote corners of the world. . . . What wage workers, tenants, and sharecroppers had in common was that they had lost access to subsistence agriculture---basic production and consumption now depended on global markets. . . . Their incomes, and quite literally their survival, were now linked to global price fluctuations over which they had no control. . . . Between 1864 and 1873 the amount of cotton that a tenant or farmer had to produce to buy a given quantity of Berar's most important food grain, jowar, doubled, and then it doubled again by 1878. Perhaps even more significant, the relative price of grains to cotton changed dramatically from year to year (changes of 20 percent or even 40 percent were not exceptional). . . . As one historian of India has remarked, "Successful participation in markets requires economic autonomy and the capacity to take risks and sustain losses. Poor and indebted peasants had neither.". . . As the colonial government of India observed in 1874, "The more the area's food stocks is diminished in favor of fibers, the greater the danger from any failure of the monsoon becomes, & the greater appears to be the necessity of some security against the consequences of such failure."

Indeed, cotton production for export typically produced a quagmire of poverty, debt, and underdevelopment well into the twentieth century. As the director of the Gharbieh Land Company in Cairo reminded his audience in a speech to an international federation of cotton manufacturers, "You have only to go to the villages and see the dwellings our people live in, their very small interest in life, their hard work from morning till evening without distractions would give you an idea as to how the Egyptian peasant lives his gloomy existence."

In 1877 and again in the late 1890s, Berar, as well as northeastern Brazil, witnessed the starvation of millions of cultivators as cotton prices fell while food grain prices rose, putting food out of reach of many cotton producers. . . . [T]he 1870s famine was not caused by a lack of food (indeed, food grains continued to be exported from Berar), but by the inability of the poorest agricultural laborers to buy urgently needed food grains. In India alone, between 6 and 10 million people died in the famines of the late 1870s. Observed one gazetteer, "Had Berar been an isolated tract dependent on its own resources, it is possible that . . . there would have been no famine." High prices had made food unavailable to many peasants and agricultural laborers, and during the 1900 famine, another 8.5 percent of the population of Berar died. . . . The British medical journal *The Lancet* estimated that famine deaths during the 1890s totaled 19 million, with fatalities concentrated in the tracts of India that had recently been recast to produce cotton for export. In the town of Risod, a contemporary observed that people "died like flies.". . . [Was it *socialism* that caused all this??]

Although our historical imaginations are usually dominated by cities, factories, and industrial workers, we have seen that much of the emergence of the modern world occurred in the countryside---by the often violent turning of rural people into the creators and consumers of commodities made or used elsewhere. This emphasis on the countryside allows for an equally important emphasis---the importance of coercion and violence to the history of capitalism. Slavery, colonialism, and forced labor, among other forms of violence, were not aberrations in the history of capitalism, but were at its very core. . . . Moreover, the fruits of the laborers' activities continue to be distributed in radically unequal ways---with cotton growers in Benin, for example, making a dollar a day or less, while the owners of cotton growing businesses in the United States have collectively received government subsidies of more than $35 billion between 1995 and 2010. Workers in Bangladesh stitch together clothing under absurdly dangerous conditions for very low wages, while consumers in the United States and Europe can purchase those pieces with abandon, at prices that often seem impossibly low (133-134, 296-297, 307-308, 326, 333-337, 441-442).

EXPLOITATION---WITHOUT RESPONSIBILITY AND WITHOUT REDRESS

From *How Europe Underdeveloped Africa* (except where noted):

In some quarters, it has often been thought wise to substitute the term "developing" for "underdeveloped." . . . However . . . it is best to remain with the word "underdeveloped" rather than "developing," because the latter creates the impression that . . . the countries of Africa, Asia, and Latin America are escaping from a state of economic backwardness . . . and that they are emancipating themselves from the relationship of exploitation. That is certainly not true, and many underdeveloped countries in Africa and elsewhere are becoming more underdeveloped in comparison with the world's great powers, because their exploitation by the metropoles is being intensified in new ways.

One . . . economist, in a book on development, accepted that the comparative statistics of the world today [1971] show a gap that is much larger than it was before. By his own admission, the gap between the developed and the underdeveloped countries has increased by at least 15 to 20 times over the last 150 years. However, the . . . economist in question does not give a historical explanation, nor does he consider that there is a relationship of exploitation. . . . Instead, he puts forward a biblical explanation!

In Africa, land . . . was robbed wholesale from Africans by colonial powers and then sold to whites at nominal prices. For instance, after the Kenya highlands had been declared "Crown Land," the British handed over to Lord Delamere 100,000 acres of the best land at a cost of a penny per acre. Lord Francis Scott purchased 350,000 acres, and the East African Syndicate took 100,000 acres adjoining Lord Delamere's estate---all at giveaway prices. . . . During the colonial era, Liberia was supposedly independent; but to all intents and purposes, it was a colony of the U.S.A. In 1926, the Firestone Rubber Company of the U.S.A. was able to acquire one million acres of forest land in Liberia at a cost of 6 cents per acre and 1 percent of the value of the exported rubber (14, 21, 154).

The Nigerian coal miner at Enugu earned one shilling per day for working underground and nine pence per day for jobs on the surface. Such a miserable wage would be beyond the comprehension of a Scottish or German coal miner, who could virtually earn in an hour what the Enugu miner was paid for a six-day week. . . . A truck driver on the famous copper belt was in a semi-skilled grade. In one mine, Europeans performed that job for 30 pounds per month, while in another, Africans did it for 3 pounds per month. . . . In Southern Rhodesia in 1949, Africans employed in municipal areas were awarded minimum wages from 35 to 75 shillings per month. . . . [B]ut white workers (on the job for 8 hours per day compared to the Africans' 10 to 14 hours) received a minimum wage of 20 shillings *per day* plus free quarters and other benefits.

In the Union of South Africa, African laborers worked deep underground, under inhuman conditions which would not have been tolerated by miners in Europe. Consequently, black South African workers recovered gold from deposits which elsewhere would be regarded as non-commercial. And yet it is the white section of the working class which received whatever benefits were available in terms of wages and salaries. Officials have admitted that the mining companies could pay whites higher than miners in any other part of the world because of the super-profits made by paying black workers a mere pittance. As is well known, those conditions still operate.

It was exploitation without responsibility and without redress. In 1934, forty-one Africans were killed in a gold mine disaster in the Gold Coast, and the capitalist company offered only 3 pounds to the dependents of each of these men as compensation (150-152).

Trading companies made huge fortunes on relatively small investments in those parts of Africa where peasant cash-crop farming was widespread. The companies did not have to spend a penny to grow the agricultural raw materials. . . . Many . . . in every section of the continent took to earning cash because they had to pay various taxes in money or because they were forced to work. Good examples of Africans literally being forced to grow cash crops by gun and whip were to be found in Tanganyika under German rule, in Portuguese colonies, and in French Equatorial Africa and the French Sudan in the 1930s. These facts came most dramatically to the attention of the outside world when Africans resorted to violence. For example, forced cultivation of cotton was a major grievance behind the outbreak of Maji Maji wars in Tanganyika and behind the nationalist revolt in Angola as late as 1960.

One of the main purposes of the colonial taxation system was to provide requisite funds for administering the colony as a field of exploitation. European colonizers ensured that Africans paid for the upkeep of the governors and police who oppressed them and served as watchdogs for private capitalists. . . . When colonial governments seized African lands . . . they created the conditions whereby landless Africans had to work not just to pay taxes but also to survive. In settler areas such as Kenya and Rhodesia, the colonial government also prevented Africans from growing [their own] cash crops so that their labor would be available directly for the whites. One of the Kenya white settlers, Colonel Grogan, put it bluntly when he said of the Kikuyu: "We have stolen his land. Now we must steal his limbs. Compulsory labor is the corollary of our occupation of the country."

In those parts of the continent where land was still in African hands, colonial governments forced Africans to produce cash crops no matter how low the prices were. The favorite technique was taxation. *Money* taxes were introduced on numerous items---cattle, land, houses, and the people themselves. Money to pay taxes was got by growing cash crops or working on European farms or in their mines.

An interesting example of what colonialism was all about was provided in French Equatorial Africa, where French officials banned the Mandja people (now in Congo Brazzaville) from hunting, so that they would engage solely in cotton cultivation. The French enforced the ban although there was little livestock in the area and hunting was the main source of meat in the people's diet.

Finally, when all else failed, colonial powers resorted widely to the physical coercion of labor---backed up of course by legal sanctions, since anything which the colonial government chose to do was "legal." The laws and by-laws by which peasants in British East Africa were required to maintain minimum acreages of cash crops like cotton and groundnuts were in effect forms of coercion by the colonial state, although they are not normally considered under the heading of "forced labor." The simplest form of forced labor was that which colonial governments exacted to carry out "public works"---building castles for governors, prisons for Africans, barracks for troops, and bungalows for colonial officials. A great deal of this forced labor went into the construction of roads, railways, and ports to provide the infrastructure for private capitalist investment and to facilitate the export of cash crops. Taking only one example from the British colony of Sierra Leone, one finds that the railway which started at the end of the nineteenth century required forced labor from thousands of peasants driven from the villages. The hard work and appalling conditions led to the death of a large number of those engaged in work on the railway.

In the British territories, this kind of forced labor (including juvenile labor) was widespread enough to call forth in 1923 a "Native Authority Ordinance" restricting the use of compulsory labor for porterage, railway and road building. More often than not, means were found of circumventing this legislation. An international Forced Labor Convention was signed by all colonial powers in 1930, but again it was flouted in practice.

The French government had a cunning way of getting free labor by first demanding that African males should enlist as French soldiers and then using them as unpaid laborers. This and other forced labor legislation known as "prestation" was extensively applied in vast areas of French Sudan and French Equatorial Africa. Because cash crops were not well established in those areas, the main method of extracting profit was by taking the population and making it work in plantation or cash-crop regions nearer the coast. Present-day [1971] Upper Volta, Chad, and Congo Brazzaville were huge suppliers of forced labor under colonialism. The French got Africans to start building the Brazzaville to Pointe-Noire railway in 1921, and it was not completed until 1933. Every year of its construction, some ten thousand people were driven to the site---sometimes from more than a thousand kilometers away. At least 25 per cent of the labor force died annually from starvation and disease, the worst period being from 1922 to 1929.

In Nigeria, it was the tin companies which benefited from the forced-labor legislation, allowing them to get away with paying workers 5 pence per day plus rations. For most of the colonial period, the French government performed the same kind of service for the big timber companies who had great concessions of territory in Gabon and Ivory Coast. The Portuguese and Belgian colonial regimes were the most brazen in directly rounding up Africans to go and work for private capitalists under conditions equivalent to slavery. In Congo, brutal and extensive forced labor started under King Leopold II in the last century. So many Congolese were killed and maimed by Leopold's officials and police that this earned European disapproval even in the midst of the general pattern of colonial outrages. When Leopold handed over the "Congo Free State" to the Belgian government in 1908, the Belgian government hardly relaxed the intensity of exploitation in Congo.

The Portuguese have the worst record of engaging in slavery-like practices, and they too have been repeatedly condemned by international public opinion. One peculiar characteristic of Portuguese colonialism was the provision of forced labor not only for its own citizens but also for capitalists outside the boundaries of Portuguese colonies. Angolans and Mozambicans were exported to the South African mines to work for subsistence, while the capitalists in South Africa paid the Portuguese government a certain sum for each laborer supplied. ([As of 1971,] the export of Africans to South Africa is continuing.)

With the minimum investment of capital, the colonial powers could mobilize thousands upon thousands of workers. Salaries were paid to the police officers and officials, and labor came into existence because of the colonial laws, the threat of force, and the use of force. . . . In most parts of Africa, the Europeans who wanted to see a railroad built offered lashes as the ordinary wage and more lashes for extra effort (157-158, 164-167, 209).

These post-slavery colonialists were nakedly demonstrating that the official end of slavery didn't mean the end of capitalism's need for the cheapest labor possible, by any means at hand or imaginable.

Africa's contribution to European capitalism was far greater than mere monetary returns. The colonial system permitted the rapid development of technology and skills within the [European centers]. It also allowed for the elaboration of the modern organizational techniques of the capitalist firm.

[W]ith colonialism, the capitalists determined what types of labor the workers should carry on in the world at large. Africans were to dig minerals out of the subsoil, grow agricultural crops, collect natural products, and perform a number of other odds and ends such as bicycle repairing. Inside Europe, North America, and Japan, workers would refine the mineral and the raw materials and make the bicycles. That international division of labor . . . insured that there would be the maximum increase in the level of skills in the capitalist nations.

The above considerations apply fully to any discussion of the military aspects of imperialism, the protection of empire being one of the crucial stimulants. The new colonial dimension to European military preoccupation was particularly noticeable in the sharp naval rivalry among Britain, Germany, France, and Japan before and during the First World War. That rivalry over colonies and for spheres of capitalist investment produced new types of armed naval vessels, such as destroyers and submarines. By the end of the Second World War, military research had become the most highly organized branch of scientific research.

The international division of labor of the colonial period also ensured that there would be growth of employment opportunities in Europe, apart from the millions of European settlers . . . already residing in Africa. Agricultural raw materials were processed in such a way as to form by-products, constituting industries in their own right. The number of jobs created in Europe and North America by the import of mineral ores from Africa, Asia, and Latin America can be seen from the massive employment rolls of institutions such as steel works, automobile factories, alumina and aluminum plants, copper wire firms, etc. Furthermore, those in turn stimulated the building industry, the transport industry, the munitions industry, and so on. [And created millions more jobs in the technology, banking, medical, marketing, consulting, education, insurance, real estate, etc. industries and government employment as well, to name just a few career opportunities considered normal and natural in the U.S. and Europe.]

But, in Africa, the mining that went on left holes in the ground, and the pattern of agricultural production left African soils impoverished. . . . [T]he non-industrialization of Africa was not left to chance. It was deliberately enforced by stopping the transference to Africa of machinery and skills which would have given competition to European industry in that epoch. . . . [G]enuine technical education [in the colonies] was ruled out because the fundamental purpose of the colonial economy did not permit the development of industry and skills within Africa. . . . [F]or the most part, whatever skilled jobs needed to be done within the restricted field of mining and industry in Africa were met by the importation of Europeans (173, 175, 177, 179, 180, 232, 251).

If there is anything glorious about the history of African colonial education, it lies not in the educational crumbs which were dropped by European exploiters, but in the tremendous vigor displayed by Africans in mastering the principles of the system that had mastered them. In most colonies, there was an initial period of indifference towards school education, but once it was understood that schooling represented one of the few avenues of advance within colonial society, it became a question of Africans clamoring and pushing the colonialists much further than they intended to go. . . . In 1930, the Governor-General of French West Africa reported:

"Each new school that is opened is immediately filled to overflowing. Everywhere, natives in their multitude are clamoring to be educated. Here, a Chief wants a school of his own, so he builds it; or again, some village or other may offer to bear the cost of fitting out a school. At certain places on the Ivory Coast, the villagers pay the teachers out of their own pockets. Our pupils often come from distances of 20 to 50 kilometers.". . .

[A]part from physical and financial sacrifices, Africans in some colonies had to wage a political battle to have the principle of African education accepted [among the] white settler populations. In Kenya, white settlers made it clear that as far as they were concerned, an uneducated African was better than an educated one, and that one with the rudiments of education was at least preferable to one with more than a few years of schooling. The Beecher report on education in Kenya (produced in 1949) . . . stated frankly:

"Illiterates with the right attitude to manual employment are preferable to products of the schools who are not readily disposed to enter manual employment.". . .

There were also a few Europeans who foresaw what were called the "dangers" of giving Africans a modern education; namely, the possibility of its leading towards freedom. Certainly, Europeans were not at all happy with any schools which were . . . not under direct colonialist control. . . . One Catholic mission report from nearby Tanganyika in 1933 warned against allowing Tanganyika Africans to set up schools controlled by themselves. It noted that: "Independent schools are causing difficulties in Kenya. Such schools may easily become hotbeds of sedition.". . . They

were considered "training grounds for rebellion.". . .
Europeans knew well enough that if they did not control the
minds of Africans, they would soon cease to control the
people physically and politically (263-265, 271-272).

THE CARIBBEAN

From *The American Slave Coast*, Ned and Constance
Sublette, 2016 (except where noted):

[T]he island colony of Saint-Domingue [Haiti] was the most
profitable piece of ground on earth, contributing perhaps as
much as 40 percent of France's annual income with its
products. In 1789 it supplied about 60 percent of the coffee
sold in the western world; only Jamaica could compete with
it as a producer of sugar; and it produced indigo, cotton, and
tobacco. It was a high-volume consumer of kidnapped
Africans; forty thousand arrived in 1789 alone, after a
six-year period that had seen Saint-Domingue's agricultural
production double. As such, it generated a vast cash flow for
the trans-African slave trade at its height. . . . The great
revenues from Saint-Domingue created the prosperity that
was the source of the power France projected
internationally. But it was not royal power; the fortunes of
the slave trade were made by the bourgeoisie [capitalist
class] (307).

After 1850 . . . [w]ith Africans selling in Havana, Cuba at
$1000 or more, the profits on such voyages were immense; a

merchant could afford to pay out bribes, and even burn the ship if necessary. [By this time, there was a broad-based ban on the transatlantic slave trade---not on slavery itself---and Britain was stopping ships on the high seas if thought to be carrying slaves.] New York merchants, especially, were involved in the financing, but a wide variety of US maritime centers participated in the trade, including Baltimore and New Orleans. W.E.B. Dubois's list, compiled from congressional documents, shows vessels from Portland, Maine; Portsmouth, New Hampshire; Boston; Rhode Island; Mystic, Connecticut; and Philadelphia (610, 612).

The 1840 census showed New Orleans . . . effectively tied with Baltimore as the second largest city in the nation. New Orleans, the number-one port in the United States, was unlike the rest of the South in many ways. It was urban. It had a substantial business community and a local economy dominated by factors [business contractors], a waterfront that shipped the world's greatest quantities of cotton and much sugar and, since the plantations of Louisiana and Mississippi required enormous amounts of credit, it had a large banking sector, heavily capitalized by captive human beings. . . . New Orleans was the largest slave market in the United States.

Anti-slavery Ohio senator Thomas Morris, in a speech of February 9, 1839, juxtaposed what he called the "slave power of the South" with what he saw as the other great evil, the "banking power of the North." "The cotton bale and the bank note," he declaimed, "have formed an alliance: the credit system with slave labor."

Meanwhile, the experience of slavery was getting worse as plantation management became more efficient. The antebellum cotton plantation of the Deep South was a much harsher regime than that of the Upper South; life as a worker there was hell on earth. Cotton planters extracted continually increasing amounts of labor through torture via a system not unlike modern time-metric monitoring of workers that Edward E. Baptist memorably calls "the whipping machine." Under this regime, failure to meet production targets was punished by vicious, lacerative whippings at the end of the long work day. And the production targets were continually increased, pushing the worker ever harder. With this abusive, efficiency-conscious system in place, cotton productivity reached levels not seen again until mechanization (507, 534).

In 1770, the North American colonies sent to the West Indies [the European Caribbean slave colonies] nearly one-third of their exports of dried fish and almost all their pickled fish; seven-eighths of their oats, seven-tenths of their corn, almost all their peas and beans, half of their flour, all their butter and cheese, over one-quarter of their rice, almost all their onions; five-sixths of their pine, oak, and cedar boards, over half their staves, nearly all their hoops; all their horses, sheep, hogs and poultry; almost all their soap and candles. As Professor Pitman has told us, "It was the wealth accumulated from West Indian trade which more than anything else underlay the prosperity and civilization of New England and the Middle Colonies" (*Capitalism & Slavery*, 108).

The [Caribbean] colonies [from the beginning of the 18th century] were obliged to send their valuable products to England only and use English ships. They could buy nothing but British unless the foreign commodities were first taken to England. [T]hey were to work for the greater glory of England . . . reduced to a state of permanent vassalage, confined solely to the exploitation of their agricultural resources. Not a nail, not a horseshoe . . . could be manufactured, nor hats, nor iron, nor refined sugar. In return for this, England made one "concession"---the colonial products were given a monopoly of the home market. (C&S, 56)

While there was no mass slavery in Europe itself, only when and where workers were strongly and broadly organized has capitalism ever conceded a human existence for labor; not necessarily slavery but as close to it as they could get it, as demonstrated in *The Enemy,* by Felix Greene (except where noted):

Britain could not have advanced her industrialization so rapidly if an abundant supply of domestic cheap labor had not been made available. Britain had been an agricultural country, but with wool becoming Britain's chief export, the landowners found raising sheep more profitable than renting land to tenants. Thousands of peasant farmers were evicted from their cottages, uprooted, often with no warning, from the land that they and their fathers had used from time immemorial.

What caused even more widespread suffering were the Acts under which public or "common land" became enclosed. In accordance with age-old tradition, all men were free to use these common lands for the grazing of sheep and goats; in the economy of the peasant farmers, access to this land was an essential element without which they could not survive. Between 1760 and 1810 no fewer than 2,765 Enclosure Acts were passed. Thus, when the new [textile] factories that were springing up required labor, tens of thousands of homeless and hungry agricultural workers, with their wives and children, were forced into the cities in search of work, any work, under any conditions, that would keep them alive (53, 54).

The cotton industry was the capitalist industry par excellence [and probably the origin of one of capitalism's defining creations: massive concentration of factory wage labor]. The size of the average cotton mill was something unprecedented in British economic history. . . . The population employed by the industry rose from 350,000 in 1788 to 800,000 in 1806 [all due to slave-produced raw cotton] (*Capitalism & Slavery*, 127-128).

The emergence of a huge, property-less and impoverished working class was precisely what the new industrialists wished for. They could, and did, dictate their own conditions.

The laboring people of Britain were subjected to treatment so inhumane that today we would have difficulty believing it if the official records were not there for us to read. For wages that would barely keep them alive, workers were herded into huge slums that had no sewerage, no adequate water supply . . . no playgrounds. . . .

Children were cheaper to hire than adults, so children frequently became the wage earners while their parents remained unemployed. Pauper children, bought from the Guardians of the Poor, were cheaper still and were shipped in groups from London to the mining towns of South Wales and the northern cotton mills. Boys of nine were sent down the mines to work for fourteen hours a day hewing coal; and in the cotton mills of Lancashire, girls of seven would work as "apprentices" from five in the morning until eight at night.

Under what were known as the "Combination Laws," all forms of collective bargaining, all associations of workers to improve their position, were considered "conspiracies" punishable by imprisonment. If the workers rioted, they were fired on by troops. When, in sheer desperation, men began to wreck the machinery, Parliament passed an act making the damaging of machinery punishable by death.

In ways such as these did those with wealth and power achieve the continuation of the supply of cheap labor (54, 55).

From *The American Slave Coast*:

[W]hite abolitionists were few in number [in the 13 colonies] in the 1830s and '40s. But many non-abolitionist white northerners were anti-slavery, less because of compassion for black people than because they saw slavery as setting an unacceptably low floor for working conditions. The sectional controversy over slavery was about its expansion to the new territories. Free labor did not want to go where there was slavery, and slave-owners felt locked out of any place where they couldn't use and sell slaves. [There was a vast market for cotton and sugar and both of these crops wore out the soil; slavery would always need land expansion to survive]. . . . In 1844, Texas was the battleground.

James Hamilton of South Carolina printed a report in the *Telegraph* . . . that presented "the Texans as a people struggling for their liberty, and therefore entitled to our sympathy," as John Quincy Adams disgustedly wrote in his diary. He continued: "The fact is directly the reverse---they are fighting for the establishment and perpetuation of slavery, and that is the cause of the south Carolinian sympathy with them." [Only two of the first ten U.S. presidents did not own slaves; both of them were named Adams] (510, 537).

Ulysses S. Grant, a junior officer in [the Mexican War], later wrote in his memoir that "I was bitterly opposed to the measure [of annexing Texas], and to this day regard the war which resulted as one of the most unjust ever waged by a stronger against a weaker nation." [Grant's quick summary]:

"Americans, who had received authority from Mexico to colonize . . . paid very little attention to the supreme government, and introduced slavery into the state almost from the start, though the constitution of Mexico did not, nor does it now, sanction that institution. Soon they set up an independent government of their own, and war existed, between Texas and Mexico, in name from that time until 1836, when active hostilities very nearly ceased upon the capture of Santa Anna, the Mexican President. Before long, however, the same people---who with permission of Mexico had colonized Texas, and afterwards set up slavery there, and then seceded as soon as they felt strong enough to do so---offered themselves and the State to the United States, and in 1845 their offer was accepted. The occupation, separation, and annexation were, from the inception of the movement to its final consummation, a conspiracy to acquire territory out of which slave states might be formed for the American Union. . . . The Southern rebellion [the Civil War] was largely the outgrowth of the Mexican war" (538-39).

US law prohibited black soldiers from enlisting in the army (though there were already black sailors in the navy), and Lincoln did not at first attempt to change it, so African American volunteers were turned down. The war went badly for the North during this time.

[With the Emancipation Proclamation], now the war could be won. . . . Emancipation meant black soldiers in combat.

Pursuant to the Proclamation, 166 black regiments were created. The number of African Americans who fought is officially around 180,000, but it seems likely there were more than that. By war's end, about 10 percent of the US Army was black. . . . [T]hey were known as dedicated fighters. For them, the war was even more dangerous than it was for white soldiers (639, 645).

Thus, ironically, Black people were principal to freeing capitalism to exploit and oppress them after the Civil War, including abandoning them to the terror of lynchings and Jim Crow only 12 years after the War ended.

The Emancipation Proclamation and the coming of the greenback were concurrent and were intimately related. Once the enormous appraised value of the bodies and reproductive potential of four million people was no longer carried on the books as assets, dwarfing other sectors of the economy on paper and generally distorting the economy, the financial revolution of a national paper money was able to happen. The end of the slave-breeding industry was crucial to the remaking of American money (640-641).

Capitalism was born, enriched, and empowered through slavery. However, after the Civil War, armed with its new and more flexible financial structure, unbuckled from the world's social pariah that slavery had become, and no longer fettered by slavery's competition for land in the continent's yet unsettled territories, capitalism took flight, with the continent itself becoming a launching pad. True to its predatory nature, once the continent was conquered from sea to shining sea and from the Great Lakes to the Rio Grande, capitalism, at the end of the 19th century, was compelled to enlarge the hunt. It set its sights on some low-hanging fruit on which Spain was losing its colonial grip, the two juiciest being the Philippines and Cuba.

From *The True Flag*, Stephen Kinzer, 2017:

Harvard's Henry Adams, ardent supporter of the war on the Philippines [1899-1902] and mentor to Henry Cabot Lodge, wrote, "I turn green in bed at midnight if I think of the horror of a year's warfare in the Philippines. We must slaughter a million or two foolish Malays in order to give them the comforts of flannel petticoats and electric railways." [Adams refers to exports U.S. capitalism intends for the Philippines to absorb. The U.S. had reached the saturation point of its home market by the end of the 19th century and its productive forces, as per the unwritten laws of capitalism, desperately needed a broader market.]

Filipinos were rebelling [against U.S. rule after the U.S. took over from Spain]. . . . The Anti-Imperialist League called a meeting in Boston where the first speaker told the packed house, "We are laying waste to the country with fire and sword, burning villages and slaughtering the inhabitants, because they will not submit to our rule."

[President McKinley gave an address in Pittsburg where he answered the anti-imperialists.] He asserted that insurgents represented only a small fraction of Filipinos; that they bore sole responsibility for the war because they had rebelled against America's legal authority and that he would not rest until he had crushed them. "They assailed our sovereignty," McKinley declared, "and there will be no useless parley, no pause, until the insurrection is suppressed and American authority acknowledged and established."

Soon after McKinley made that vow, Admiral Dewey, the hero of Manila Bay [where the U.S. defeated Spain for the "right" to rule the Philippines, as well as Cuba and Puerto Rico] returned home from the Philippines to a welcome the like of which no American had ever seen. Congress ordered a special medal struck with his image. In Boston, a 280-voice choir greeted him with Handel's "See the Conquering Hero Comes." New York celebrated him for three days. He circled Manhattan in the *Olympia*, his flagship during the Battle of Manila, and marched at the head of a festive parade.

The visual centerpiece of this parade was the triumphal Dewey Arch, a newly built monument intended as tribute to the conqueror---and to the idea of American conquest. Designed over a period of months by twenty-eight sculptors and architects, the arch spanned Fifth Avenue at Twenty-Fourth Street. It was modeled after the first-century Arch of Titus in Rome but was more ornate. A double colonnade led past allegorical sculpture groups, including a pair called "East Indies" and "West Indies" that showed grateful natives sitting submissively beneath towering female figures symbolizing the United States. The arch was adorned with reliefs depicting "Call to Arms," "Progress of Civilization," "Protection of Our Industries," and "Return of the Victor." It was crowned, one hundred feet above Fifth Avenue, with a statue of winged Victory, standing tall in a vessel pulled by four steeds and holding a laurel wreath above her head. TO THE GLORY OF THE AMERICAN NAVY AND IN GREETING TO OUR ADMIRAL, said the inscription.

Dewey passed under his arch to the cheers of a vast crowd on September 30, 1899. A couple of days later he paraded through Washington with President McKinley at his side. Afterward, the two men met at the White House. McKinley presented Dewey with a golden sword crafted by Tiffany & Co (142-143, 151-152).

Some Americans refused to join the hero worship set off by Dewey's return. Activists from across the country gathered in Chicago to found the American Anti-Imperialist League, which was to subsume all local groups and direct a national civic uprising. Its platform was a single demand: Congress must withdraw American troops from the Philippines and "concede to them the independence for which they have so long fought and which of right is theirs." The convention's climax was a speech called "The Policy of Imperialism":

The Philippine War was as unnecessary as it is unjust---a wanton, wicked, and abominable war . . . and what is the answer? "No useless parley! More soldiers! More guns! More blood! More devastation! Kill, kill, kill! And when we have killed enough, so that further resistance is stopped, then we shall see." Translated from smooth phrase into plain English, this is the program. . . . In the vocabulary of our imperialists, "order" means above all submission to their will. Any other kind of order, be it ever so peaceful and safe, must be suppressed by a bloody hand."

In December of that year, 1899, at a session of the Senate, Albert Beveridge stood to passionately report on his tour of the Philippines:

"Thanksgiving to Almighty God that He has marked us as His chosen people!" Beveridge cried as he began. Then, methodically and persuasively, he crystallized essential arguments for taking the Philippines. "No land in America surpasses in fertility the plains and valleys of Luzon," he said, referring to the largest island in the archipelago. He talked of rice, coffee, sugar, coconuts, hemp, tobacco, "mountains of coal," forests that "can supply the furniture of the world for a century to come," and "great deposits" of gold.

Beveridge went on to assert that the Philippines would become America's base for China trade, "the mightiest commercial fact in our future;" that its harbors and ports would make "military and naval operations" possible over a vast area; and that the entire archipelago would become "a fortress thrown up in the Pacific, defending our Western coast, commanding the waters of the Orient, and giving us a point from which we can instantly strike and seize the possessions of any possible foe." Then, in a rising crescendo, he argued that the imperative was not simply commercial and strategic but spiritual: to rule people of "a barbarous race" was America's right and duty.

Beveridge spoke for two spellbinding hours. When he was finished, the Senate gallery erupted in applause. Newspapers around the country reported his words under banner headlines. . . . [H]e became a national figure almost overnight. Columnists and editorial writers praised him. . . . The Republican National Committee printed a million copies of his speech. Congratulatory letters flooded into his office. . . . Imperialism had a dynamic new champion (153-154, 156-158).

[But subduing the resistance in the Philippines would require far more than high-sounding speeches, even the most reactionary.] General MacArthur wrote in a dispatch [in direct contradiction to President McKinley's claim that insurgents represented only a small fraction of Filipinos] that the insurgency represented "almost complete unity of action of the entire native population." McKinley . . . summoned his cabinet and reviewed the bad news from the Philippines. All agreed that it was time for a change of strategy. . . . Secretary of War Elihu Root told reporters in Washington that the United States Army would henceforth follow a "more rigid policy" in the Philippines. One commander announced ominously that he had ordered his officers to begin using "European methods." Reports of this change in strategy filled front pages around the country. . . . President McKinley [just re-elected] had reached a peak of popularity. In a speech on September 5, 1901, he declared that subduing foreign lands so they must trade with the United States was the way to sell "our increasing surplus." "Our capacity to produce has increased so enormously, and our products have so multiplied, that the problem of more markets requires our urgent and immediate attention." "The expansion of our trade and commerce is the pressing problem."

Despite renewed efforts at press censorship, news about excesses committed by soldiers appeared regularly in American newspapers. [As a result,] the senate convened the Committee on the Philippines on January 26, 1902. Secretary of War Root wrote to the Committee: "The war on the part of the Filipinos has been conducted with the barbarous cruelty common among uncivilized races." "[It] has been conducted by the American Army with scrupulous regard for the rules of civilized warfare, with careful and genuine consideration for the prisoner and the non-combatant, with self-restraint and with humanity never surpassed, if ever equaled, in any conflict, worthy of praise and reflecting credit on the American people."

[But] General Robert Hughes, who had commanded units in several parts of the Philippines, testified that he routinely ordered the burning of Filipino villages in order to deny shelter to insurgents. Under questioning, Hughes responded that the destruction was [also] a punishment: The women and children are a part of the family, and where you wish to inflict a punishment, you can punish the man probably worse in that way than in any other.

Under questioning, one defendant, Major Anthony Waller, revealed . . . that while he was serving in a reprisal campaign on Samar, General Smith had given him extermination orders. "I want no prisoners," Smith had told him. "I wish you to kill and burn. The more you kill and burn, the better you will please me. I want all persons killed who are capable of bearing arms in actual hostilities against the United States." "Persons ten years and over are those designated as being able to bear arms." Smith then ordered that Samar "be made a howling wilderness." His officers and men complied. According to their own testimony, they razed every village they found, usually massacring civilians.

In his first appearance before the Committee, General Smith denied that he ever gave orders to kill. Later testimony showed that this was a lie. Once caught, Smith reveled in the truth. . . . [H]e proclaimed loudly that he had meant every word. That guaranteed his conviction. Secretary Root let him off with a reprimand on the grounds that he had been driven to excess by "cruel and barbarous savages." Major Waller was acquitted. Many cheered. General Funston, a national hero, was disgusted by the prosecution of his fellow officers. During a speaking tour at the beginning of 1902 designed to drum up support for the war, he declared, "I personally strung up thirty-five Filipinos without trial, so what was all the fuss over Waller's dispatching a few treacherous savages?"

The United States Army waged its last large campaign in the Philippines in the first months of 1902 under General

Franklin Bell. Bell's orders: all natives must be forced from their homes into fortified camps; "neutrality should not be tolerated," so natives not actively aiding the U.S. force must be killed; crops must be burned and livestock destroyed; and a native would be selected by lot for execution every time an American was killed. . . . The rebel force went hungry and ran out of ammunition. Starvation and diseases spread. . . . That marked the effective end of Filipino resistance. Fifty-four thousand civilians died during Bell's three-month campaign. . . . An American decree made it a crime for any Filipino to advocate independence.

On July 1, 1902, Congress passed the Philippine Organic Act providing a legal structure by which the United States could rule the islands indefinitely. Three days later, on July 4, President [Theodore] Roosevelt [who, as vice-president, became president in 1901 when McKinley was shot] issued a proclamation declaring the Philippine War officially over and thanking American soldiers for their "self-control, patience, and magnanimity.". . . The Philippine War lasted forty-one months. . . . Commanders later estimated that they killed about twenty thousand Filipino insurgents. Hundreds of thousands of civilians also perished. The population of water buffalo, the essential article of rural life in the Philippines, fell by 90 percent. Americans suffered 4,234 dead and 2,818 wounded. During those forty-one months, far more Filipinos were killed, or died as a result of mistreatment, than in three and a half centuries of Spanish rule (194, 196, 208, 216-217, 220-225).

The main reason Americans were reluctant to allow Cuban independence [in 1901] transcended race. Lodge, Roosevelt, and their friends had come to realize that Cuban revolutionaries wanted not just independence but also sweeping social reform. If they were allowed to rule Cuba, they would not do what the Americans wanted. Three of their main goals were anathema to the United States: they proposed to limit the amount of land foreigners could own in Cuba, seize large plantations and parcel them out to peasant families, and impose tariffs on imported goods to encourage local business. The biggest landholders in Cuba were American fruit and sugar companies. American investors were digging mines, building railroads, and establishing power companies in Cuba. Exporters counted on the Cuban market. If *Cuba Libre* meant an end to all that, *Cuba Libre* could not be.

Congress worked to legalize a peculiar form of independence. On February 25, 1901, Senator Orville Platt, chairman of the Senate Committee on Cuban Relations, introduced a bill to make Cuba a new kind of colony, not officially annexed like Hawaii, Puerto Rico, Guam, and the Philippines, but just as fully under Washington's control. Until its repeal more than thirty years later, the Platt Amendment set the paradigm by which the United States dominated Central America, the Caribbean, and many lands farther away: formal independence, rule by natives who cooperated with American businessmen, and military intervention as necessary. This was a giant conceptual leap beyond the classic colonialism that European powers had practiced for centuries, based on direct rule by foreigners. It became a template for American dominance of weak countries. Latin Americans called it *Plattismo*. [We know it today as "neo-colonialism." It also relieved the U.S. of the cost of direct colonial administration.]

The Platt Amendment was . . . a pillar of "the large policy." [It] affirms Cuba's right to independence, but only under conditions "substantially as follows":

---The government of Cuba shall never enter into any treaty or other compact with any foreign power or powers which will . . . permit [them] to obtain by colonization or for military or naval purposes, or otherwise, lodgment in or control over any portion of said Island.

---The government of Cuba consents that the United States may exercise the right to intervene for the preservation of Cuban "independence" [my quotations].

---The government of Cuba will sell or lease to the United States lands necessary for coaling or naval stations at certain specified points, to be agreed upon with the President of the United States.

"There is, of course, little or no independence left Cuba under the Platt Amendment," General Leonard Wood, the military governor of Cuba, wrote in a letter from Havana.

Later, a rebel hero, Maximo Gomez, stated that he wished he had never agreed to American intervention in Cuba. "None of us thought that it would be followed by a military occupation of the country by our allies, who treat us as a people incapable of acting for ourselves, and who have reduced us to obedience, to submission, and to a tutelage imposed by force of circumstances," Gomez wrote. "This cannot be our fate after years of struggle [against Spanish colonialism]" (189, 191, 192).

BANKS

From *Dollar Diplomacy*, Scott Nearing and Joseph Freeman, 1925:

The Bolivian Loan of 1922 is an excellent illustration of the type of bankers' contract frequently met with in the case of Latin-American loans. . . . As a guarantee that the loan . . . will be repaid, the Republic of Bolivia . . . "pledge[s] the following shares of stock, funds, revenues and taxes as security for the full payment of the principal, premium, and interest on [the loan]:

A. "All of the shares . . . of the Banco de la Nacion Boliviana belonging to the Republic and which the Republic represents are sufficient at present to control said Bank." . . . Should the capital stock of the Banco de la Nacion be increased at any time during the life of the loan, "the Republic shall acquire such proportion of additional shares as shall be necessary for said control; the shares so acquired shall immediately thereafter be pledged as security for the loan.". . . In addition to these shares of the bank stock, the Republic pledges, as security for the loan:

B. All revenues representing dividends on these shares of stock.

C. The tax upon mining claims or concessions.

D. Revenues from the alcohol monopoly.

E. Ninety per cent of the revenue received by the Republic from the tobacco monopoly.

F. The tax on corporations other than mining and banking.

G. The tax upon the net income of the bank.

H. The mortgage tax.

I. The tax on the net profits of mining companies.

J. All import duties.

K. All export duties.

L. All funds, revenues, and taxes now or hereafter allocated by special laws to the construction of the Potosi-Sucre Railroad.

M. First mortgages and liens upon all the properties and earning of the Railroads constructed from Villazon to Atocha and from Potosi to Sucre, including their franchises and other property and their net earnings.

For the practical administration of the provisions contained in the Bolivian Loan Contract, a Permanent Fiscal Commission is provided, consisting of three members. "The President of the Republic shall appoint the three Commissioners; of these, two to be appointed upon recommendation of the Bankers.". . . The Commission "shall act by majority vote; and shall elect as its chairman and Chief Executive one of the two Commissioners who shall have been recommended by the Bankers." This Bankers' representative . . . "shall be elected a member of the Board of Directors of the Banco de la Nacion Boliviana, and the Republic shall take such action as may be necessary to secure his election and continuance in office as such."

As for the duties of the Commission, they are simple and inclusive. So long as any bonds of the loan remain outstanding . . . "the collection of all taxes, revenues, and income of the Nation shall be supervised and fiscalized by the Permanent Fiscal Commission.". . . Should a default take place, the members of the Commission automatically become the central figures in the Bolivian political [and economic] world (30-34).

From *OPEN VEINS*:

The siphoning off of national resources . . . is [also] largely explained by the recent proliferation of U.S. branch banks pushing up their heads throughout Latin America like mushrooms after rain. . . . According to the International Banking Survey, today [1971] First National City alone has 110 branches scattered through seventeen Latin American countries. . . . Chase Manhattan Bank acquired the Banco Lar Brasileiro (34 branches) in 1962, the Banco Continental (42 branches in Peru) in 1964, the Banco del Comercio (120 branches in Colombia and Panama) and the Banco Atlantida (24 branches in Honduras) in 1967, and the Banco Argentino de Comercio in 1968. . . . [I]n 1968 alone more than seventy U.S. bank affiliates were opened in Central America, the Caribbean, and the smaller South American countries.

No one knows the precise extent of the simultaneous growth of parallel activities---subsidiaries, holding companies, finance companies, agencies. . . . This banking invasion has served to divert Latin American savings to the U.S. enterprises established in the region. . . . The public relations departments of the various U.S. banks operating abroad unblushingly announce that their chief aim in the countries in which they operate is to channel internal savings into the multinational corporations which are their head offices' clients. . . . U.S. banks dispose of Latin America's national savings at their pleasure.

President Kennedy has already admitted that, in 1960, "from the under-developed world, which needs capital, we took in $1,300,000,000 and we sent out in capital for investment $200,000,000."

In taking out many more dollars than they bring in, the enterprises whet the region's chronic dollar hunger; the "benefited" countries are decapitalized instead of capitalized. And here the loan mechanism of international credit organizations goes to work. . . . The IMF and the World Bank put more and more pressure on Latin American countries to reshape their economies and finances in terms of payment of the foreign debt. But the fulfillment of commitments . . . gets more and more difficult and at the same time more necessary. . . . To pay off these debts, new injections of foreign capital are resorted to, generating bigger commitments, and so on and on. Servicing the debt consumes a growing proportion of income from exports, which [then] cannot finance the necessary imports; new loans to enable the countries to supply themselves thus become as indispensable as air to the lungs.

The so-called free play of supply and demand in the international market does not exist; the reality is a dictatorship of one group over the other. . . . Latin American underdevelopment is not a stage on the road to development, but the counterpart of development elsewhere (223-224, 226-227, 236, 245).

There are those who turn to the comfortable "conventional wisdom" that is handed down to us to "explain" the massive breadth of 3rd World destitution: that it is caused by corruption by their government leaders. U.S. politicians never tire of expressing their umbrage over "corruption" by any regime they want vilified. No doubt corruption is innate and endemic to capitalism and can be found almost everywhere and there's also no doubt many of the U.S.' most favored 3rd World strongmen are lavishly feathering their nests.

But one is hard pressed to understand how someone can look at the sea of poverty in virtually every country in Latin America, every country in Africa, and nearly every country of Asia, and somehow conclude that they each are, and have been for the last four generations, corrupting themselves into this never-ending morass of suffering rather than that they have been systematically (and forcibly) drained by the world's powerful, with no chance of making capitalism benefit the vast majority of their own people. Yet they are forced to live under its grinding economic dictates as per their assigned position in capitalism's lopsided world order. Which is what keeps them poor and weak---with or without corruption.

This, from an article in an October 13th, 2018 issue of *The Economist* magazine, is a case in point:

On the campaign trail, Imran Khan, Pakistan's new prime minister, presented himself as the man to break the country's addiction to "hand-outs" from the West. Whereas previous governments used to go begging to the IMF [International Monetary Fund] for funds, he said, his Pakistan Movement for Justice would focus instead on recouping billions of dollars hidden from the taxman abroad.

[These tax havens are mainly used by international corporations to keep their profits from being taxed.] After less than two months in office, on October 8, Mr. Khan reversed himself. His finance minister announced that the government would, after all, be seeking a big loan from the IMF.

The previous government . . . lifted annual GDP growth to a ten-year high of more than 5%. But it did so on the back of expensive imports of fuel and machinery, even as its determination to prop up the Pakistan rupee hurt export industries such as textiles. The result has been dramatic growth in the current-account deficit since early 2016. Foreign-exchange reserves have fallen sharply as a result. They currently stand at $8 billion, which is not enough to cover the expected bill for imports and foreign-debt repayments until the end of the year. To keep the lights on (literally---many of Pakistan's power plants run on imported coal), the government needs to find around $10 billion in short order.

Even Mr. Khan could see that Pakistan was going to need a loan. But for the past few weeks he has desperately been seeking alternatives to an IMF bail-out. In a televised address, he asked all Pakistanis living abroad to donate $1,000 apiece to the government. . . . To show that government funds wouldn't be wasted, he has engaged in public displays of austerity. The government has auctioned off eight buffaloes kept to provide milk for the prime minister's residence, along with 61 luxury cars.

As Mr. Khan hunted for benefactors, investors panicked. The stock market had its biggest daily drop in a decade on October 8th. The delay . . . has weakened Mr. Khan's hand in negotiations with the IMF over the terms of any loan. . . . [T]he Fund is likely to push for further devaluation of the rupee, increased tax collection and higher interest rates. . . . If Mr. Khan was unsure of it before he assumed power, he must surely now realize that Pakistan's problems run deeper than corrupt leadership. And if voters were unsure of it before they cast their ballots, they are quickly discovering that Mr. Khan, for all his self-assurance and star power, cannot fix things quite as quickly or easily [or at all] as he promised.

Actually, if one is looking for corruption in Third World countries, one need look no further than any one of the many heavyweight masters of global corruption. From a *Business Report* article of Feb. 6, 2000:

Cigarette giant British American Tobacco encouraged and relied on smuggling to boost sales in Latin American countries . . . according to internal company memos [dating from the early to mid-1990s] in which senior executives discussed the role of smuggling in building market share and profits. . . . Cigarette smuggling cheats governments of taxes and import fees. . . . [G]overnors of 20 Columbian states were preparing a lawsuit against the industry to recover tax losses resulting from smuggling. They would be following the lead of Canada, which in December filed a one billion dollar lawsuit against RJ Reynolds Tobacco, accusing it of involvement in a smuggling operation that undercut a government program to discourage smoking through higher taxes.

Likewise, a September 17, 1998 *CNN Money* report, citing *The Los Angeles Times*, says:

Philip Morris and British-American Tobacco are charged with setting prices and dividing market share in Argentina, Venezuela, Costa Rica and other Latin American countries. Internal documents cited in the lawsuit describe the deals as well as the involvement of some of the firms' top executives, the report said.

At about that same time, *The Economist* magazine, after reviewing the same internal documents, said they "showed that the big tobacco multinationals colluded to fix prices in as many as 23 countries in Africa, Asia, the Middle East, Latin America and Europe."

From *Open Veins* (except where noted):

[Latin America] is a vast region with an enormous *potential* market and a *real* market shrunken by the poverty of its masses. The consumers to whom big auto and refrigerator plants direct their products are only 5 percent of the Latin

American population. Hardly one in four Brazilians can really be considered a consumer.

The abyss that exists in Latin America between the well-being of the few and the misery of the many is infinitely greater than in Europe or the United States. Hence, the methods necessary to maintain it are much more ruthless. . . . *In Latin America, civil liberties are incompatible with free enterprise.*

Fresh from taking power [in Argentina in 1976,] the Videla dictatorship hastened to ban strikes and decree freedom of prices while putting wages behind bars. . . . When the regime was a year old the real value of wages had fallen by 40 percent. The feat was accomplished by terror. "Fifteen thousand disappeared, 10,000 jailed, 4,000 dead, tens of thousands exiled---that is the naked balance sheet of the terror," as the writer Rodolfo Walsh totted it up in an open letter. Walsh sent the letter on March 29, 1977, to the three chiefs of the governing junta. On the same day, he was kidnapped and disappeared.

[T]he dictators are not self-taught: they have learned the techniques of repression and the arts of government at academies run by the Pentagon in the United States and the Panama Canal Zone (251, 272-274, 276).

Robert McNamara, when Secretary of Defense [1961-1968] . . . informed a Congressional committee:

"Probably the greatest return on our military assistance investment comes from the training of selected officers and key specialists at our military schools in the United States and overseas. These students are hand-picked by their countries to become instructors when they return home. They are the coming leaders, the men who will have the know-how and impart it to their forces. I need not dwell upon the value of having in positions of leadership men who have first-hand knowledge of how Americans do things and how they think. It is beyond price to us to make friends of such men" (*The Enemy*, 136).

[In Brazil], [w]hen the [1964] coup took place against [moderate reformer] Goulart, the United States had in Brazil its largest embassy anywhere on earth. Lincoln Gordon, the ambassador, admitted to journalists thirteen years later that his government had long been financing the forces opposing [Goulart's] reforms. "What the hell," said Gordon, "that was more or less a habit in those days. . . . The CIA used to dole out political funds." In the same interview, Gordon explained that when the coup took place the Pentagon had a huge aircraft carrier and four supply ships stationed off the Brazilian coast "in case the anti-Goulart forces should ask for our help." That help, he said, "wouldn't be just moral. We would back them up logistically, with supplies, munitions, oil" (272-273).

In June, 1973, a coup d'état in Uruguay dissolved the parliament, put unions outside the law, and banned all political activity. This brought in a murderous 12-year military dictatorship whose main benefactor was the U.S. The regime's promises to improve the economy were dashed by the 1973 global oil crisis. Uruguay started borrowing money from international lenders, chiefly from the US. The opening of the small local economy to global corporations and financial institutions ruined local Uruguayan companies, who could no longer compete. The regime was forced to borrow even more and cut budget expenditures. By 1981, the country of 3 million people owed 4 billion dollars (*Latin American Dictators of the 20th Century*, 134).

What are the Latin American coups d'état but successive episodes in a war of pillage?

The bishops of France have spoken [Déclaration de Lourdes, October 1976] about [the world order]: "We, who belong to nations purporting to be the world's most advanced, form a part of those who benefit from exploitation of the developing countries. We do not see the sufferings that this inflicts on the flesh and spirit of entire peoples. We help to reinforce the division of the present world in which the domination of poor by rich, of weak by strong, is conspicuous. . . . Do we perhaps not understand that the militarization of poor countries' regimes is one of the consequences of economic and cultural domination by the industrialized countries? (273-274, 279)

In 1912, Woodrow Wilson, an avowed promoter of peace, won the presidency. Wilson preached the supreme value of self-determination, which he called the right of all people "to choose the sovereignty under which they shall live." In office, though, he sent American troops to intervene in Cuba, Haiti, the Dominican Republic, Mexico, and Russia. No other president invaded as many countries as this sworn promoter of self-determination. Like his predecessors---and successors---Wilson insisted that he was doing it for the good of the targeted countries (*The True Flag*, 232).

Also in 1912, still-president William H. Taft declared: "The day is not far distant when . . . the whole hemisphere will be ours in fact as, by virtue of our superiority of race, it already is ours morally." Taft said that the correct path of justice in U.S. foreign policy "may well be made to include active intervention to secure for our merchandise and our capitalists opportunity for profitable investment."

And did it ever include that!

Early in [the 20th] century, banana enclaves made their appearance in [Central and South America]. . . . [T]he "bananization" of Guatemala, Honduras, Costa Rica, Panama, Colombia, and Ecuador suggests that it is a tree of hell. United Fruit became owner of the biggest latifundio in Colombia when a big strike broke out on the Atlantic coast in 1928. Banana workers were mowed down with bullets in front of a railroad station. "The forces of public order are authorized to punish with the aid of appropriate weapons," it was officially decreed, and no further decree was necessary to wipe the massacre from official memory.

Massacres were continual throughout the area. In Guatemala in 1933, Dictator Jorge Ubico shot one hundred trade union, student, and political leaders while restoring the laws against Indian "vagrancy." Each Indian had to carry a book listing his days of work; if these were deemed insufficient, he paid the debt in jail or by bending his back over the ground without pay for half a year. On the unhealthy Pacific coast, men worked up to their knees in mud for $.30 a day and United Fruit explained that Ubico had forced it to cut wages. . . . Ubico was swept off his pedestal in 1944 by a revolution. Juan Jose Arevalo, elected to the presidency of Guatemala, instituted a vigorous education plan and a new labor code to protect rural and city workers. Trade unions sprang up; United Fruit, the virtually untaxed and uncontrolled owner of vast lands and of the railroad and port, was no longer omnipotent on its domains. . . . Highways and the new port of San Jose broke United Fruit's monopoly of transport and export. . . . [S]ince United Fruit was using a mere 8 percent of its land, which extended from ocean to ocean, its unused lands began to be distributed to the peasants. A frenetic international propaganda campaign was launched: "The Iron Curtain is falling over Guatemala," roared the radio, newspapers, and the bigwigs of the Organization of American States. Colonel Rodolfo Castillo Armas, a graduate of the Fort Leavenworth [Kansas] military post, invaded his own country with troops trained and equipped for the purpose by the United States, and with support from U.S.-piloted F-47 bombers.

Foreign intervention was followed by a series of ferocious dictatorships in Guatemala. . . . [A]grarian reform was blown to smithereens when Castillo Armas fulfilled his mission of returning the land to United Fruit and other expropriated landlords. . . . Indiscriminate repression formed a part of the military "search and destroy" campaign against guerrilla movements. All the men of the village of Cajon del Rio were exterminated; in Agua Blanca de Ipala they were burned alive after being shot in the legs. A rebellious peasant's head was stuck on a pole in the center of San Jorge's plaza. . . . In the cities, the doors of the doomed were marked with black crosses. Occupants were machine-gunned as they emerged, their bodies thrown into ravines. "We had to get rid of a Communist government which had taken over," Dwight D. Eisenhower said nine years later (106-109, 112-115).

[In Mexico] in 1910, 800-odd latifundistas, many of them foreigners, owned almost all the national territory. . . . Of a population of 15 million, 12 million depended on rural wages. . . . With the worker tied by inherited debts or by legal contract, slavery was the actual labor system. . . . In a report on his visit, John Kenneth Turner wrote that "the United States has virtually reduced [the Mexican dictator] Diaz to a political dependency, and by so doing has virtually transformed Mexico into a slave colony of the United States." U.S. capitalism made big profits directly or indirectly from its association with the dictatorship. "The Americanization of Mexico of which Wall Street boasts," wrote Turner, "is being accomplished with a vengeance."

Mexico's hour of revenge struck in 1910: the country rose in arms against Diaz behind Emiliano Zapata, most loyal to the cause of the poor. . . . For agricultural communities throughout Mexico, the last decades of the nineteenth century had been a period of ruthless pillage. . . . Sugar haciendas dominated the life of the state. . . . A law in 1909, providing further seizure of land from its legitimate owners, was the last straw.... The men of the south quickly formed a liberating army.

Diaz fell. . . . The struggle went on for nearly ten years. . . . Zapata denounced "the infamous pretension" of reducing everything to a mere change of men in government: the revolution was not being made for that. . . . The agrarian reform proposed to "destroy at the roots and forever the unjust monopoly of land, in order to realize a social state which guarantees fully the natural right which every man has to an extension of land necessary for his own subsistence and that of his family." [M]aximum limits were laid down for holding sizes, according to climate and fertility. . . . A system of local democracy put the reins of political power and of economic maintenance in the people's hands. Zapatista schools sprouted and spread . . . and an authentic democracy took shape and gained in strength. . . . Bureaucrats and generals no longer imposed methods of production and of living. . . . In the spring of 1915, all the fields [of the state of] Morelos were under cultivation, mostly with corn and food crops. . . . Zapata's life ended in 1919. A thousand men lying in ambush fired into his body. . . .

These long war years in Mexico were also years of continual U.S. intervention: the Marines staged two landings and several bombardments, and diplomatic agents framed a variety of political plots. . . .

[Ultimately, as we know,] Mexico did not . . . achieve its goals of economic independence and social justice. . . . The fading of the bright banners has been studied by a variety of scholars. Edmundo Flores writes [50 years later, in 1970] in an official publication that "at the present time, 60 percent of Mexico's total population has incomes below $120 a year and goes hungry." Eight million Mexicans consume almost nothing but beans, corn, tortillas, and chilis (120-125).

General Smedley Butler had spent decades leading invasions of other countries. He commanded troops in Cuba and the Philippines, fought the Boxers in China, helped overthrow the governments of Nicaragua and Honduras, directed occupations of the Dominican Republic and Haiti, secured the Panamanian regime that gave Americans the right to build their canal, and won a Medal of Honor---the first of two---for valor in suppressing Mexican resistance at Veracruz. By the 1920s he was a living legend, a personification of "the large policy." The Marine Corps decided to use his popularity as a recruiting tool and sent him on a speaking tour. It did not unfold as planned. Butler strayed far from his script. He not only failed to defend the policies for which he had fought, he denounced them. . . . In passionate speeches and articles, he said that serving as a marine commander had made him "a high-class muscle man for big business" and "a gangster for capitalism."

"I helped make Mexico and especially Tampico safe for American oil interests in 1914. I helped make Haiti and Cuba a decent place for the National City Bank boys to collect revenues in. I helped in the raping of half a dozen Central American republics for the benefit of Wall Street. I helped purify Nicaragua for the International Banking House of Brown Brothers in 1902-1912. I brought light to the Dominican Republic for the American sugar interests in 1916. I helped make Honduras right for the American fruit companies in 1903. In China in 1927 I helped see to it that Standard Oil went on its way unmolested. Looking back on it, I might have given Al Capone a few hints. The best he could do was to operate his racket in three districts. I operated on three continents" (The True Flag, 235-236).

From *The Inevitable War*, Francis Delaisi, 1911

Today [1911], the great European nations are governed by men of affairs: bankers, manufacturers, export merchants. Their aim is to find everywhere markets for their rails, their cotton goods, their capital. Throughout the world they struggle for the control of the railways, loans, and mining concessions, etc. And if, perchance, two rival camps cannot agree, they make an appeal to arms.

Thus we saw the Japanese fight with the Chinese in 1895 for the exploitation of Korea; in 1898 the Americans battled with the Spaniards for the right to exploit Cuba. In 1899

England fought with the Boers for the possession of the Transvaal [South Africa] mines; in 1900 all Europe invaded Peking to force the Chinese to accept their railroads; and finally, in 1904 the Japanese and the Russians slaughtered each other for 18 months to determine whose should be the right to exploit Manchuria.

Five wars in ten years! . . . None of these wars resulted in conquest [or annexation]: Manchuria will always be a part of the Celestial Empire [China]; China has kept its Emperor; South Africa is an autonomous political unity; and Cuba is an independent republic [if only in name]. But their railroads, their loans, their import duties are all the booty of the victors.

Our great modern financial oligarchies are not looking for subjects but customers; they do not wage "patriotic" wars in the old sense. These men of affairs wage commercial wars.

But now a conflict is brewing compared to which the horrible slaughter of the Russo-Japanese War will be child's play.

All over the world the English capitalists are struggling with the German capitalists and the only visible means of deciding the rivalry is war---provided the working classes of both countries do not revolt.

During the entire 19th century England held undisputed sway in the commercial world. It was said of her: "She is a block of iron on a block of coal." She had an abundant supply of iron to manufacture engines and the coal which is necessary to drive them. She could therefore better than all other nations develop an incomparable industry. And the sea which surrounds her on all sides permitted her to build an unequalled navy.

And thus throughout the 19th century the spinners and weavers of Manchester and the steel-mills of Birmingham spread over the whole world their cotton goods, cloths, hardware, their rails and locomotives, realizing without great effort enormous profits.

France, already dropping behind, was the only state offering even weak competition. . . . But then an unexpected rival arose. Up to 1870 Germany had been an almost exclusively agricultural country; but her soil was poor and annually 300,000 Germans emigrated to distant America, seeking a more fertile soil which might nourish them.

. . . All this changed after the war [Franco-Prussian War of 1870-71, won by the Prussians (Germans)]. [After that, German leader] Bismarck . . . had only one idea: to make of his country a great industrial nation like Great Britain.

Gradually on the banks of the Rhine, in Westphalia, in Saxony, in Silesia, great blast furnaces, steel mills and forges arose; millions of spindles turned in the cotton mills; woolen mills, chemical industries, and great shipyards sprang up as if by magic. The railways of all the small states were placed under one management; the government dredged the streams and built canals; the admirably constructed harbors were fitted up in the best possible way and soon a constantly growing merchant marine began carrying the flag and the merchandise of the [German] Empire to all quarters of the globe.

Then the English began to grow uneasy. At first they had watched the efforts made by the heavy Saxons to copy their industry with a disdainful smile. They asserted and believed that the Germans manufactured only trash.

However, this "trash" soon overwhelmed them. In order to rid themselves of it they passed a law requiring all articles of German manufacture to bear the trade mark: "Made in Germany." They hoped thus to discredit their rivals. But . . . [consumers] discovered that a very large number of excellent articles which had until then been thought to be the best products of English industry, came directly from [Germany]. . . . Instead of discrediting them they had given them an advertisement! . . .

At the same time, from all the principal markets of the globe, the English consuls who supervise the international commerce sent disquieting reports to London. From all sides they reported the presence and activity of German traveling salesmen, engineers and contractors who were getting all the orders and taking up concessions and loans. A consul in Syria wrote to his government: "Once upon a time all the European products used here were purchased in England. Today I am writing to you on a table manufactured in Germany, with a German pen, on German paper. Soon the only thing English left will be myself."

On all sides, the progress of British commerce became less marked; that of German commerce was disquietingly rapid.

Naturally the Kaiser supported the efforts of his merchants and bankers with all the resources at the disposal of his diplomacy. Everywhere his ambassadors worked for concessions and orders for his countrymen. Colonies were founded in Africa; railways were built across China; the mines of Chile were exploited, etc.

It was especially Turkey upon which the people of Berlin cast their eyes. In 1903, William II obtained from the Sultan Abdul-Hamid the concession of the Baghdad railway of which there is so much talk in the press at present. It is a question of a stretch of 2000 miles of railroad running from Constantinople to the head of the Persian Gulf---a matter of nearly 200 million dollars. One may easily imagine what great revenue such an enterprise will bring to the bankers, steel magnates and manufacturers beyond the Rhine.

But it developed that this German railroad terminated in Mesopotamia in a region hitherto considered by the English as their own commercial preserve. And, moreover, this railway can in a few days transport Turkish troops into the neighborhood of Bombay and thus threaten the British domination in India.

Then the English capitalists began to tremble. Their initial surprise was changed to uneasiness and then developed into fury.

Today, in all quarters of the globe, in the Balkan Peninsula, in Turkey, from Persia to China, in Central America, in Brazil, from Argentine Republic to Chile, the bankers of Berlin and London, the ship-owners of Liverpool and Hamburg, the Captains of Industry in Glasgow and Essen, are involved in a struggle.

To defend at least the colonial commerce, Mr. Chamberlain, the head of the Birmingham steel magnates, proposed a protective tariff; but this proposal, which would have increased the cost of living, was rejected en masse by the English working-men. After this the great capitalists who govern England saw only one solution.

It would be necessary at all costs to hold a reckoning with this unexpected rival who was about to threaten the British prestige in all the markets of the world. Since the industrial competition could not be decided by peaceful means, an appeal would have to be made to Dreadnoughts and cannon. It is towards this goal that the English government is working with remarkable unanimity (19-31).

In this fratricidal strife not one centime of French money, not one drop of French blood [should] be risked. We shall say to both [England and Germany]: not a penny! Not a single soldier! That is doubtless what [the French population] would say, if it were consulted.

Unfortunately, [the French people are] not asked for advice. In spite of the outward democratic form, everyone knows that the people neither govern nor control the governors. A small band of capitalists has taken hold of all the departments of the administration and of the great financial undertakings; they hold in their hands all the banks, mines, railways, companies, in short all the economic furniture of France. . . . They have the entire press that molds public opinion in their pay. Skillfully hidden behind the screen of democracy, they are in reality the masters of the destinies of the country. . . .

It must be hoped that a sudden change in the public opinion and the fear of a revolution may put a halt to the doings of these men before their dangerous intrigues succeed. But we must bear in mind that this sudden change in public opinion will not take place unless the people are warned in time.

The financial coterie which is carrying on their machinations in the dens of the chancelleries is not large, but it has a most powerful ally: the popular ignorance. The great words of Honor, the Fatherland, the Flag, the National Defense, in the name of which for centuries crimes have been committed, and unjust and useless wars waged, are always powerful in the ears of the masses. . . .

It is against this revival of chauvinistic passions that we must defend ourselves. For there is only one means of informing the people as to the true situation in Europe: accustom them to discern the intrigues of commercialists underlying diplomatic differences; show them beneath the high-sounding words Honor, Fatherland, National Safety, the orders, concessions, and loans that are the real moving forces of wars. And then, when they are asked to stake their lives on the plains of Belgium to assure Creusot his dividends, there will be such an upwelling of popular feeling, not only among the workmen but also in the peasant and middle classes, that the financial oligarchy will recoil and these men of prey will halt on the threshold of crime. The only hope of peace left to us is to dare to tell the truth to men of courage (95, 97, 115, 119).

In 1919, in the immediate aftermath of the horrendous slaughter of WW I, Frank Vanderlip, president of National City Bank and former Assistant Secretary of the Treasury, spoke at the Radcliffe Club in New York City. He was explaining why he wouldn't (nor would the U.S.) endorse the proposed League of Nations meant specifically to prevent another such war:

We must all be guided by intelligent self-interest---that is, interest for our people and an eagerness to progress, and a League of Nations or a similar document would not encourage such progress. We must have an incentive for progress, and competition with other nations is the greatest and, in fact, the only incentive in trade relations [!!] (*All The Presidents' Bankers*, 62).

From *DOLLAR DIPLOMACY*, 1925:

American investments in the Near East, chiefly in tobacco and oil, have turned that section of the world into an

American "sphere of influence." The extent to which the government at Washington has been willing to back up American investors in that region is described in the following statement issued by the United States Bureau of Naval Intelligence:

"We have extensive interests in the Near East, especially in tobacco and petroleum. Early in 1919 several American destroyers were ordered to Constantinople for duty in the Near East. . . . The possible development of the economic resources of this part of the world was very carefully investigated by representatives of American commercial interests. These representatives were given every assistance by the Navy, transportation furnished them to various places, and all information of commercial activities obtained by the naval officers in their frequent trips around the Black Sea given them. . . . The Navy not only assists our commercial firms to obtain business, but when business opportunities present themselves, American firms are notified and given full information on the subject. . . . One destroyer is kept continually at Samsun, Turkey, to look after the American tobacco interests at that port. . . . The American tobacco companies represented there depend practically entirely on the moral effect of having a man-of-war in port to have their tobacco released for shipment" (66-67).

[At the end of the 19th century], oil was discovered along the Gulf Coast of Mexico. The first oil ever produced in Mexico in substantial quantities . . . began to flow on May 14, 1901. . . . Edward L. Doheny and a group of American capitalists had secured . . . an estate covering 280,000 acres. . . . Later, the same men obtained an adjoining 150,000 acres. . . . Within a decade, Mexico had risen from a position of no importance in the oil world to be, next to the United States, the largest producer of petroleum. By 1920, Mexican production exceeded the combined production of all oil fields in the world outside of the United States. By 1910, therefore, it was evident that the oil fields of Mexico were one of the richest economic prizes in the world.

It was during these same years---1905-1915---that the development of the internal combustion engine and the use of fuel oil under marine boilers had led British statesmen and businessmen to undertake a worldwide quest for oil reserves. The Doheny interests soon had powerful rivals.

On assuming office in 1913, President Woodrow Wilson found himself facing a Mexico torn by civil war, with Huerta in power . . . ready to continue the old policy of Diaz. Part of this policy was to favor the British oil interests headed by Lord Cowdray's syndicate. "That the Huerta forces have maintained the Diaz policy of antagonism to American oil interests and friendship to Lord Cowdray is apparent," one observer stated at that time. . . . "It is a rich prize for which these American and British capitalists are contending."

The nature of the interest which the leading powers held at this time in Mexican oil was described by Edward L. Doheny, as follows: "Inasmuch as both Germany and Great Britain are seeking and acquiring sources of supply for large quantities of petroleum, it seems to me that there can be no question but that the United States must avail itself of the enterprise and ability and pioneer spirit of its citizens to acquire and to have and to hold a reasonable portion of the world's petroleum supplies. If it does not, it will find that the supplies of petroleum not within the boundaries of United States territory will be rapidly acquired by citizens and Governments of other nations." [Is there any question but that the natural impulse of global capitalism *always* leads toward war?]

The conviction that [Mexican president] Huerta was friendly to British oil interests led to a long-drawn-out policy of political intrigue, financial strangulation, moral eloquence, and finally armed intervention, the consistent aim of which was to drive Huerta from Mexican politics. Latin Americans who were led by President Wilson's pre-election speeches and writings to believe that during his administration they would be free to govern themselves without North American interference, were quickly disillusioned. . . . [When asked in an interview by British statesman, Sir William Tyrell] ". . . to explain [his] Mexican policy . . . President Wilson . . . said in his most decisive manner: 'I am going to teach the South American Republics to elect good men!'"

"The present policy of the Government of the United States is to isolate General Huerta entirely," Secretary Bryan cabled the American diplomatic representatives on November 24, "to cut him off from foreign sympathy and aid and from domestic credit, whether moral or material, and to force him out. It hopes and believes that isolation will accomplish this end and shall await the results without irritation or impatience. If General Huerta does not retire by force of circumstances it will become the duty of the United States to use less peaceful means to put him out.". . . Those who had land, mineral, industrial and oil investments in Mexico were crying so loudly for intervention that President Wilson declared: "I have to pause and remind myself that I am President of the United States and not of a small group of Americans with vested interests in Mexico."

[In April, 1914, President Wilson declared that] ". . . a series of incidents have recently occurred which cannot but create the impression that the representatives of General Huerta were willing to go out of their way to show disregard for the dignity and rights of this Government and felt perfectly safe in doing what they pleased.". . . Wilson was kept in touch with every official communication from Mexico; nevertheless, he misstated the facts surrounding three trivial incidents in such a way as to rouse national excitement and asked Congress to approve his using "the armed forces of the united States in such ways and to such an extent as may be necessary to obtain from General Huerta and his adherents the fullest recognition of the rights and dignity of the United States."

The President's message called forth a flood of patriotic oratory in Congress. . . . On April 21 . . . marines and bluejackets landed at Vera Cruz, seized the cable office, post office, telegraph office, customs house, and railroad station, and on the following day American forces "commenced advance to take the entire city at eight o'clock under guns of war vessels.". . . The capture of Vera Cruz cost the United States the lives of seventeen marines and bluejackets. It cost Mexico the lives of two hundred men, women and children. . . . On the same day, the wife of the American Charge d'Affaires at Mexico City wrote, "We are certainly isolating and weakening him at a great rate. 'Might is right.' We can begin to teach it in the schools."

[At a conference to settle these affairs], the U.S. proposed a program that, as President Wilson made clear, unless accepted by Mexico peacefully, would be forced upon her by arms. The American delegation declared: (1) that a Constitutionalist [one of the opposition forces supported by the U.S.] be made provisional president of Mexico, (2) that the election board shall contain a Constitutionalist majority, (3) that the land and naval forces of the United States shall remain in Mexico for an indefinite time, and extend to the elections. This was tantamount to controlling Mexico's elections through armed force, as the United States had done in Santo Domingo [Dominican Republic] and Nicaragua (85-110, not all pages included).

In Nicaragua, as in Santo Domingo, and Haiti as well, the strategic interests of American diplomats and the financial interests of American bankers combined to produce first diplomatic and later military intervention. The strategic considerations centered around plans for a United States naval base at Fonseca Bay, and, more important still, a canal route across Nicaragua to supplement the advantages of the Panama Canal.

The government of President Jose Santo Zelaya opposed attempts on the part of the United States to extend its control over Nicaragua by obtaining Fonseca Bay and a canal route, as well as attempts by American business interests to establish themselves in the republic.

In 1909, a revolution against Zelaya broke out. . . . The American consul in Nicaragua at Bluefields knew about the revolution in advance, wiring the State Department on October 7 that it would break out the next day and that the new government would appeal "to Washington immediately for recognition.". . . Five days later the consul was able to report to Washington that a provisional government had been established with General Juan Estrada at the head, that this government was "friendly to American interests," and that it guaranteed "annulment of all concessions not owned by foreigners."

Steamers of the United Fruit Company and other American vessels bearing the Nicaraguan flag transported men and munitions for the revolutionists with the knowledge and assistance of the State Department representatives in Central America. . . . The government troops, however, defeated the insurgents and forced Estrada to retreat. . . . At once American marines landed . . . and with the support of American bayonets they were able to seize power. . . . A week later, Estrada . . . entered Managua, the capital of Nicaragua.

On October 27, 1910, aboard an American battleship, the principal leaders of the Estrada "revolution" signed a series of agreements later known as the Dawson Pact. These stipulated that the United States would recognize the "revolutionary" [my quotation marks] government which it had assisted to seize power on the following conditions:

1. That a constituent assembly be chosen at once which would elect Estrada president and Adolfo Diaz vice-president, for two years. Estrada could not succeed himself and no Zelayists could enter the administration.
2. That a mixed commission, satisfactory to the United States Department of State, be appointed to settle claims. . . .
3. That Nicaragua would solicit the good offices of the American Government to secure a loan to be guaranteed by a certain percent of the customs receipts collected in accordance with an agreement "satisfactory to both governments."

Secretary Knox forwarded copies of the Santo Domingo loan convention and of the proposed loan conventions with Honduras and Liberia, saying the Honduras convention would "answer all the requirements of the present case." He further instructed the American minister that "the Government of Nicaragua is to proceed at the earliest possible date to the signature of a convention with the United States which shall authorize the contemplated bankers' loan contract" to be secured by a percentage of the customs receipts.

For a time the Dawson Pact was kept secret, but the defeated Liberals in Nicaragua obtained a copy and published it. The terms upon which General Estrada was supported by the United States aroused a storm of opposition in Nicaragua. Many patriotic elements saw in the Dawson Pact, with its provisions for a loan and American control of customs, the establishment of a virtual protectorate. American control of elections aggravated the situation. In February, 1911, the American minister in Nicaragua cabled to Secretary Knox that "the natural sentiment of an overwhelming majority of Nicaraguans is antagonistic to the United States, and even with some members of Estrada's cabinet I find a decided suspicion, if not distrust, of our motives." President Estrada, he added in another wire, dated March 27, was "being sustained solely by the moral effect of our support and the belief that he would unquestionably have that support in case of trouble."

The chief aim of supporting Estrada against the opposition of the Nicaraguan people was the floating of the loan and the control of customs to secure the loan. In April the Nicaraguan National Assembly determined to adopt a constitution guaranteeing the independence of the republic and directed against foreign control through loans. This constitution was opposed by the American representatives, and when it was adopted against their opposition, Estrada dissolved the assembly and called for new elections. The step was approved by the State Department at Washington. These proceedings resulted in protests which led to the resignation of Estrada in favor of vice president Adolfo Diaz.

But Diaz was no more popular than Estrada, and American support was necessary to keep him in office. "I am assured," the American minister wired the State Department on May 11, "the Assembly will confirm Diaz in the presidency according to any one of the . . . plans which the Department may indicate. . . . A war vessel is necessary for the moral effect." On May 25 he wired that "rumors have been current that the Liberals are organizing a concerted uprising all over the country with the declared object of defeating the loan." The Liberals, he added, were "in such a majority over the Conservatives" that he hastened to repeat the suggestion "as to the advisability of stationing permanently, at least until the loan has been put through, a war vessel at Corinto." Secretary Knox replied that Diaz should not be permitted to resign and that a warship had been ordered to Nicaragua.

Secretary Knox ordered the American charge d'affaires to keep the Nicaraguan legislature in session until the loan agreement . . . was approved. . . . The charge d'affaires cabled Knox that the "opposition to these loan contracts and concessions is becoming more determined."

The State Department replied on September 30: "You are instructed that, of the Nicaraguan matters under consideration by the Department, the ratification of the pending loan contract and the amendment of the decree establishing a claims commission are of the first importance and should be disposed of before attention is directed to other subjects.". . . The Nicaraguan assembly approved the loan contracts on October 9. . . . From December 11, 1911 on, [the U.S.] collected the entire customs duties of Nicaragua.

On March 26, 1912, [American bankers] entered into an agreement with Nicaragua for a supplementary loan. . . . It was to be secured by the customs revenues, second only to the 1911 loan; by a lien on all government railway and steamship lines. . . . Proceeds of any sale of railways or steamships . . . were to be used for the repayment of the loans under this agreement. Anything left over was to be used for repaying the 1911 loan. This agreement also provided that Nicaragua should transfer all its railway and steamship lines to a corporation to be organized in the United States and to be tax free. . . . Pending repayment, the American bankers were to manage and control the railways and steamship lines exclusively and to choose the board of directors. These loan negotiations were carried on jointly by the State Department and the bankers.

Meanwhile, the unpopularity of President Diaz increased. He was able to stay in power only because of American support. . . . On July 29, [the Liberals] proclaimed a revolution, seizing a large store of war materials, a part of the railway and steamers, and several customs houses. The American manager of the Bank of Nicaragua . . . wired to Brown Brothers and Company, in New York, for protection. Brown Brothers and Company replied that the State Department advised them that Major Smedley Butler would arrive from Panama with American marines. On August 15 Major Butler landed with 412 marines, half of whom were quartered at the bank. On September 4, 1912, the State Department notified the American minister at Managua that "the American bankers who have made investments in relation to railroads and steamships in Nicaragua, in connection with a plan [loan] for relief of the financial distress of that country, have applied for protection." The American marines at once took drastic action against the revolutionists. According to the 1913 report of the United States Secretary of the Navy, eight naval vessels with 125 officers and 2600 men participated in the subjugation of the revolution. . . . The leader of the revolutionary forces surrendered to the U.S. and was exiled to Panama aboard the U.S.S. Cleveland. . . . Following the defeat of the revolutionists an election was held in which the American marines guarded the polls. On November 2, Diaz was re-elected for a term of four years.

The expenses incurred during the revolution forced Diaz to apply to the American bankers for another loan. The terms on which the bankers offered to make the loan were protested by Diaz as harsh, but they were backed up by the State Department, and were incorporated in the loan agreement on November 4, 1912. [The loan was] to be secured by the tobacco and liquor taxes, which were to be collected by the American-controlled Bank of Nicaragua. . . . [Among other harsh conditions], if Nicaragua defaulted, the bankers had the right to sell the Bank of Nicaragua and the railroad stock. . . . The bank and railroad were each to have nine directors. Six were to be named by the bankers, one by the Secretary of State of the U.S., and two by Nicaragua (151-158, 160-165, 167).

"AID," FOREIGN INVESTMENT, AND DEBT

From *The Enemy* (except where noted):

"We should take pride," says former Under Secretary of State (1961-66) George W. Ball, "in the American businessmen who, with vigor and a spirit of adventure, are investing their capital in foreign lands."

This---and Mr. Ball must know it---is sheer nonsense. "Adventure" implies risk, but thanks to "foreign aid" [as well as to the draconian terms of loans as described earlier] the risk that the U.S. businessman is taking in investing abroad is reduced to a minimum. In negotiating the foreign aid program the United States always bears in mind the necessity of opening up private investment possibilities and normally aid is given only on condition that such private investment is protected. Furthermore, special funds have been set up under aid programs to guarantee U.S. businessmen against the loss of their capital investment, profit, and interest. AID makes it almost certain that U.S. businessmen won't lose (130-131).

[Further, as Laurence H. Shoup points out in his book, *Wall Street's Think Tank*]:

[W]hen the Mexican government was threatened with default in 1995, President Clinton's new secretary of the treasury, Robert E. Rubin, and his team immediately put together a rescue plan worth $40 billion, an unprecedented amount. The goal was to fully reassure transnational capitalists and their markets that there would be no default ever. The result furthered corporate globalization by assuring capitalists that they would be bailed out no matter what risky speculative bets they made. Meanwhile, flows of private capital to emerging markets continued to accelerate (*Think Tank*, 177).

The primary objective [of military aid] in Latin America is to aid . . . in the continental development of indigenous military and paramilitary forces capable of providing, in conjunction with police and other security forces, the needed domestic security. The amount of money used through the various aid programs for [Third World] economic development is reduced to insignificance when compared to the prodigious amount poured out for military "aid." 90 percent of all foreign aid expenditures between the end of the Marshall Plan [1951] and 1963 went into one form or another of "military assistance.". . . [T]he greatest threat to America's position in the underdeveloped countries is the resistance of the poor and exploited populations who are kept in feudal conditions of oppression by the local rulers. It is in the economic interest of the American corporations who have investments in these countries to maintain this social structure. It is to keep these rulers in power that the United States has, through its assistance programs, provided them with the necessary military equipment, the finance, and training. But the feudal conditions, the unequal distribution of land, the vast disparity between the great wealth of the few and the appalling poverty of the many, are creating ever growing tensions and ever louder demands for social justice. This, in turn, means that still further military "aid" must be provided for the governments who are struggling to maintain that *status quo*.

Such an AID project was a loan to Guatemala for the purchase of fifty-four Ford cars specially equipped for fighting guerrillas. (The archbishop was photographed giving his public blessing to these Ford cars in the Central Plaza of the capital.) AID also gave 300 bullet-proof vests to the Guatemala police. Of the Guatemala budget, $12 million on average is spent annually on buying U.S. military equipment, most of it surplus. Meanwhile, Guatemala has an illiteracy rate of 75 percent and the average per capita wage is less than $200 a year.

[Further], there is another aspect of foreign military assistance, namely its effect on future U.S. sales of armaments. . . . The weapons that the government supplies under the AID program . . . stimulate the subsequent demand for weapons. Mr. Eugene Black, former president of the World Bank, described what this can mean for the manufacturer:

"Over the years, a considerable portion of our assistance has been in military hardware. This has naturally helped to orient national defense establishments toward American equipment, and the influence on exports has now become apparent. . . . U.S. military sales abroad amounted to less than half a billion dollars in 1960. Yet a recent official forecast predicts defense industry exports of $5.4 billion yearly by 1967. It forecasts a minimum market of $10 billion by 1971 and considers a potential market of $15 billion a reasonable expectation.". . .

"Assisting" foreign countries can be a very paying proposition (134-136, 138, 199).

All underdeveloped countries receiving aid from imperialist countries are chronically in debt because with aid received their indebtedness continually increases. It is a giant millstone around their necks preventing economic advance. . . . *In 1966, 44 percent of all aid flowing from the advanced to the underdeveloped countries was utilized merely to finance past and present debts.* Some of them are in a worse predicament, finding themselves in the fantastic position of paying out more to the United States in interest on past indebtedness than they are receiving in "aid."

Why are the underdeveloped countries unable to meet these interest charges? Why are they not able gradually to pay off their past indebtedness and free themselves from this oppressive burden? The answer is simple---*because they cannot.* Foreign aid must be paid off in the currency of the country that has granted "assistance." The only way of accumulating such currency is to attain a surplus of exports over imports. Since World War II the income received by the underdeveloped areas for their exports is largely controlled by the very countries that have granted them the "aid" and which, of course, find it in their interests to keep these prices as low as possible.

Aside from the enormous interest payments to the United States government, there are the still greater amounts payable abroad to U.S. corporations to cover the huge profits that they have made on their investments. These profits must also be paid in the currency of the investing country.

[F]or every dollar of foreign exchange earned by Mexico by the sale of products abroad, sixty cents has to be earmarked for the servicing of her foreign debt and for interest payments and profit of foreign investors. This leaves Mexico with only forty cents for her own essential imports---a situation true, to a greater or lesser extent, in all underdeveloped countries. Unable to accumulate sufficient capital for their own industrial and economic development, the underdeveloped countries, though providing enormous wealth for the investing countries, are kept in a permanent state of stagnation, mass poverty and subjection.

With insufficient foreign currency to pay the interest charges, they are compelled by their Washington "benefactor" to *continue borrowing*, and go still deeper into debt. . . . Increasing their total indebtedness merely tightens the economic stranglehold of the richer country. Just as a loan shark . . . prefers to keep his victims permanently in debt rather than have his loan repaid, so the chronic indebtedness of the underdeveloped countries unquestionably suits the United States [and other] imperialist countries. Through debt their control of the poorer countries can be maintained.

But what about the huge amounts of capital that have been poured into the underdeveloped countries by foreign business corporations? What about the factories that these corporations have set up, the plantations and mines and oil wells that they have developed? Surely this . . . development of their resources must be helping these countries? The answer is the same as with the so-called "aid" programs. Foreign investment has not helped the underdeveloped countries because it is not intended to help them. It is intended to make *profit* for the investors---which is a very different thing.

How *little* foreign-owned manufacturing enterprises help the local economy to earn the needed foreign exchange is seen in these figures: in 1965, U.S.-owned manufacturing firms in Latin America exported to the U.S. only 1.8 percent of their products and sold only 5-7 percent to other foreign countries; but they sold 92.5 percent of their products locally which, of course, did not bring into that country any foreign currency. Thus, far from helping a country accumulate foreign currency, foreign enterprises as we have seen, will extract it in the way of profits and interest that must be remitted abroad [as well as monopolizing the local market]. . . . Again, the primary objective of foreign investment is not to help the underdeveloped country but to rob it. (143-145, 148-149, 173).

THE WEALTH OF THE SUBSOIL---IT'S NOT JUST OIL

From *Open Veins*:

Planes cannot be built without aluminum, and aluminum cannot be produced without bauxite: the United States has almost no bauxite. Shortages of zinc cause increasing anxiety: over half comes from abroad. One-third of its iron and all of its manganese are imported. Nor has it any nickel or chrome of its own to produce jet engines. Tungsten is needed to make special steels and one-fourth of that is imported. The United States buys abroad one-fifth of the copper it uses. . . . Chile has the world's greatest reserves of copper, a third of all those now known. . . . And Chilean workers are cheap. . . . The average wage in Chilean mines in 1964 was barely one-eighth of the basic Kennecott refinery wage in the United States, although the workers' productivity was the same.

In 1964, Che Guevara showed . . . that [former dictator] Batista's Cuba was not merely sugar: the [U.S.'] blind fury against the revolution was better explained, he thought, by Cuba's big deposits of nickel and manganese. The United States' nickel reserves subsequently fell by two-thirds when Nicaro Nickel was nationalized. President Johnson threatened an embargo on French metal exports if the French bought nickel from Cuba.

[Before the Fidel Castro-led 1959 overthrow of Cuba's U.S-backed Batista regime] only a third of Cuba's population had regular jobs and half of the sugar estate lands were idle acres where nothing was produced. Thirteen U.S. sugar producers owned more than 47 percent of the total area planted to cane. . . . The subsoil wealth ---nickel, iron, copper, manganese, chrome, tungsten---formed part of the United States' strategic reserves and were exploited in accordance with the varying priorities of U.S. defense and industry. In 1958, Cuba had more registered prostitutes than mine workers.

Most of the tin refined in the world is consumed in the United States. . . . The tin can is as much the emblem of the United States as the eagle or apple pie. But the tin can is not merely a "pop" symbol; it is also . . . a symbol of silicosis: Bolivians die with rotted lungs so that the world may consume cheap tin. . . . In the cemetery at Catavi . . . a forest of white crosses stand over small graves scattered among the dark headstones of adults. Of every two children born in the mining camps, one dies soon after opening its eyes. The other, the survivor, will surely grow up to be a miner. And before he is thirty-five he will have no lungs. . . . [H]alf of Bolivia's children do not attend school and, of every ten Bolivians, six still cannot read. . . . When the violent rains pour from low clouds over Llallagua . . . one sees the unemployed crouching beside the dirt roads to collect the tin as it washes down. . . . The camps are a huddle of one-room dirt-floor shacks. . . . [T]he water supply is collective: people must await the moment of its arrival and hurry with gasoline tins and pots for a place in the queue at the public trough.

Minerals had much to do with the fall of Cheddi Jagan's socialist government in British Guiana which at the end of 1964 had again won a majority of votes. The country, now called Guyana, is the world's fourth producer of bauxite and Latin America's third producer of Manganese. The CIA played a decisive role in Jagan's defeat. Arnold Zander, leader of the strike that served as a provocation and pretext to deny electoral victory to Jagan, afterward admitted publicly that his union had dollars rained upon it from one of the CIA foundations. The new regime---very Western and very Christian---guaranteed the Aluminum Company of America [ALCOA] against any danger to its interests in Guyana.

[T]here is a clear link between the imperative need for strategic minerals . . . and the massive purchase of land . . . in Brazil's Amazonia . . . which under an agreement signed in 1964 had already been flown over and photographed by the U.S. Air Force [using instruments to detect mineral deposits in the subsoil]. . . . Before 1967, according to *Time,* foreign capitalists had bought, at $.07 an acre, a tract larger than Connecticut, Rhode Island, Delaware, Massachusetts, and New Hampshire put together.

This growing dependence on foreign supplies produces the growing identification of the interests of U.S. capitalists . . . with U.S. national security.

The U. S. government always makes common cause with private oil [and other major] corporations. Examples abound in both recent and remote history. Irving Florman, U.S. ambassador to Bolivia, reported to the White House's Donald Dawson on December 28, 1950: "Since my arrival here I have worked diligently on the project of throwing Bolivia's petroleum industry wide open to American private enterprise, and to help our national defense program on a vast scale." He went on: "I knew that you would be interested to hear that Bolivia's petroleum industry and the whole land is now wide open for free American enterprise."

Standard Oil of New Jersey, a typical multinational corporation, earns its biggest profits abroad, with Latin America bringing in more than the United States and Canada together: south of the Rio Grande its profit rate is four times higher. In 1957, more than half of its global profits came from its Venezuelan affiliates; in the same year, Shell's Venezuelan affiliates accounted for half of Shell's world profits.

In Venezuela, in half a century, oil rigs have extracted an income double the resources of the Marshall Plan. The population has multiplied by three and the national budget by 100, but most of the people scramble for the plush minority's leavings, still as poor as when the country depended on cacao or coffee. The capital, Caracas, has grown 700 percent in thirty years: the old city of airy patios, central plazas, and silent cathedrals is covered with skyscrapers as Lake Maracaibo is covered with oil wells. Today it is a supersonic, deafening, air-conditioned nightmare, a center of oil culture that might pass as the capital of Texas. . . . From surrounding hillside hovels made of garbage, half a million forgotten people observe the scene of plenty. . . .

[T]he profits milked from this wonderful cow, in proportion to capital invested, are only comparable with those obtained by old-time slave merchants and pirates. No country has yielded as much for world capitalism in so short a time: the wealth drained from Venezuela, according to Domingo Alberto Rangel, exceeds what the Spaniards took from Potosi or the English from India (134-138, 145, 148-150, 158, 164, 166).

And from *The Enemy* (except where noted):

"Here in Venezuela," said a U.S. businessman quoted by *Time* Magazine, "you have the right to do what you like with your capital. This right is dearer to me than all the political rights in the world!" [Here is a clear and rare statement of the exact nature of the "freedom" that capitalism and its politicians really mean when they invoke that time-tested pretext for imposing itself on another country.] And no wonder! *Time* goes on to say:

"Profits are enormous. So much money can be made so easily in real estate in Caracas that a speculator would be a fool to piddle around with 10-12 percent profits in industry and commerce. Fifty percent seems to be the minimum acceptable."

[Secretary of State] John Foster Dulles even held up the [U.S.-backed] Jiminez [military] regime (one of the bloodiest, and finally ousted in 1958 by popular protest) as an example for other Latin American countries to follow: "Venezuela has adopted . . . the policies which we think other countries of South America should adopt. Namely, they have adopted policies which provide a climate which is attractive to foreign capital."

And the U.S., along with other top capitalist countries, is now dead set on resurrecting that "climate" since it was interrupted by the 1999 election of President Hugo Chavez, and now his elected successor, as well. President Trump has already casually threatened to invade the country (reportedly out of an urgent, heartfelt concern for the health and welfare of the Venezuelan people).

Today [1970], dominant Western nations have acquired control of more than three-quarters of the known major mineral resources in Asian, African, and Latin American countries, and about four-fifths of the total output of twenty-two kinds of important raw materials in these same countries (158, 160, 192).

In Guatemala [in the early 1950s], 98 percent of the land was owned by 142 foreign corporations. As a step towards correcting this situation, Arbenz, the popularly elected president (72% of the vote), instituted a mild land reform program. This involved taking over 200,000 acres of *idle* land owned by the United Fruit Company. Little did he know what the consequences of this were to be. The land was not confiscated, but was to be paid for with 25 year bonds. The Guatemalan Government, as the basis for compensation, accepted the valuation of the land that the United Fruit Company itself had made for purposes of taxation---namely $600 thousand. Though this was the company's own valuation, it was rejected as not being "just compensation" and the United States Government on behalf of the United Fruit Company entered a claim for $16 million.

The actions of the Guatemalan Government were looked upon with extreme disfavor in Washington and on June 18, 1954 a Guatemalan Colonel, Castillo Armas, invaded Guatemala from neighboring Honduras. The United States supplied the arms and military equipment as well as planes and pilots. The Arbenz Government was overthrown. In Washington, Secretary Dulles declared that the success of this wholly criminal invasion added "a new and glorious chapter to the already great tradition of the American States."

That the U.S. was directly responsible for this invasion and overthrow . . . cannot be doubted. . . . The "justification" for it (as could be expected) was that "international communism" had "gained a political base" in Guatemala. [Another way of howling that the "rights and freedoms" of their *property* had been trampled on, even as that property, such as it was, had been part of the strangulation of the Guatemalan people.]

After the coup, the military junta suspended the land reform program, disenfranchised the "illiterate masses" and seized the property of peasants. All the lands expropriated from the United Fruit Company were restored to the company. The junta also abolished the taxes on dividends and profits payable to investors living outside the country.

For the record: John Foster Dulles, U.S. Secretary of State at the time, had for a long time been the legal adviser to the United Fruit Company; his brother Allen Dulles, Director of the CIA at the time, had been president of the United Fruit Company; Henry Cabot Lodge, the U.S. Ambassador to the United Nations at the time, was on the Board of Directors of the United Fruit Company; John Moors Cabot, then Assistant Secretary of State for Inter-American Affairs, was a large shareholder in the United Fruit Company; and Walter Bedell Smith, Director of the CIA before Dulles, became the president of the United Fruit Company after the Arbenz Government was overthrown. The day after the invasion, an urgent request was made by the Guatemalan Government that the United Nations Security Council be called into session to deal with the events. The request was turned down by the then President of the Security Council, who happened to be the aforementioned Mr. Henry Cabot Lodge (196-198).

In 1965, a "sugar country," the Dominican Republic, was invaded, this time---according to their commander, General Bruce Palmer---by 40,000 U.S. Marines ready "to stay indefinitely in this country in view of the reigning confusion." The vertical drop in sugar prices had been a factor in setting off popular indignation; the people rose against the military dictatorship, and U.S. troops arrived promptly to restore order. They left 4,000 dead in battles fought by patriots, body to body, in a crowded Santo Domingo slum. . . . After the invasion, President Lyndon Johnson's special envoy to the

Dominican Republic was Ellsworth Bunker, the chairman of the National Sugar Refining Company (*Open Veins*, 77-78).

Cuba under Batista was a happy hunting-ground not only for the gambling syndicates, the crooked real estate operators, the hotel owners, bar keepers, prostitutes and pimps, but for investors also. The economic hold that the United States had over the Cuban people can be judged by these figures. Prior to the [1959] revolution, the United States controlled:

80% of Cuban utilities

90% "   "   mines

90% "   "   cattle ranches

(almost) 100% "   "   oil refineries

50% "   "   public railways

40% "   "   sugar industry

25% "   "   bank balances

United States firms received 40 percent of the profits on sugar, a crop that represented 89 percent of all Cuban exports. None of this benefited Cuba. In 1957, U.S. firms employed a shade over 1 percent of the Cuban population. . . .

Conditions in Cuba . . . were no worse than in many other Latin American countries, and U.S. exploitation just as rampant. (70 percent of Brazil's principal industries are foreign-owned.). . .

John F. Kennedy said in a [1960] speech in Cincinnati while campaigning for president:

". . . We refused to help Cuba meet its desperate need for economic progress. . . . We used the influence of our Government to advance the interests and increase the profits of the private American companies which dominated the island's economy. . . . Administration spokesmen publicly hailed Batista, hailing him as a staunch ally and a good friend at a time when Batista was murdering thousands, destroying the last vestiges of freedom and stealing hundreds of millions of dollars from the Cuban people. . . . Thus it was our own policies, not those of Castro, that first began to turn our former neighbor against us" (139-140).

As Carlos Fuentes expressed [in response to Kennedy's 1961 failed invasion of Cuba at the Bay of Pigs in an attempt to reverse the revolution]:

"You killed women and children in Playa Giron [Bay of Pigs]. You bombed the first decent houses, the first schools, the first hospitals of Cubans who never before, during the long American "protectorate" over Cuba, had a roof, an alphabet, or their health. And you did it in the name of liberty, democracy, and free enterprise. What do you want us to think of these nice sounding words when in their names a population is murdered and the first proofs of concrete welfare are destroyed?" (311).

On April 16, 1953, President Eisenhower declared: "Any nation's right to a form of government and economic system of its own choosing is inalienable . . . Any nations' attempt to dictate to other nations their form of government is indefensible." (Do we listen to the words or watch the actions?) (197).

On Korea (and Japan)

There are several sources that confirm the following report on the Korean War. We've relied mainly upon what is today considered one of the most authoritative books, *The Korean War: A History*, 2010, by Bruce Cumings. We've also included (where noted) some other writers' descriptions of the pertinent Korean history, and of the War, much of which is also confirmed in Cumings' book.

In 1905, Korea succumbed to Japanese rule. This was a brutal occupation and, in 1910, Japan annexed it as a colonial possession and kept it until its defeat at the end of WWII. But a major revolt for Korean democracy occurred on March 1, 1919, when a declaration of independence was read in Seoul. Two million Koreans participated in 1,500 protests. The Japanese viciously put down the democracy movement. More than 7,500 people were killed and 16,000 were injured. Japan enacted a typical colonial regime that exploited the natural resources and the labor power of the people, transferring them to wherever they needed their labor, including to Japan itself.

Twenty-five years later, near the end of World War II as Japan was weakened, Korean "People's Committees" formed all over the country and Korean exiles returned from China, the US, and Russia to prepare for independence and democratic rule. On September 6, 1945, these disparate forces and representatives of the People's Committees proclaimed a Korean People's Republic (the KPR) with a progressive agenda of land reform, rent control, an eight-hour work day and minimum wage among its 27-point program.

But the KPR was prevented from becoming a reality. Instead, right after World War II, and without any Korean consultation, the US, fearful that the Soviets would avail themselves of the opportunity to take over all of the country [the Soviets, as well as the Chinese, shared a border with the north of Korea] offered the Soviet Union a deal to divide Korea into two nations "temporarily" as part of its decolonization. The four allied powers, including Britain and France, agreed that Japan should lose all of its colonies and territories [almost all in the Pacific Rim] and that in "due course" Korea would be free. The U.S. proposed to divide the country on the 38th parallel, which kept the capital city, Seoul, south of the line, where the U.S. would govern. To the U.S.' surprise, the Soviets accepted the partition. . . .

[After their dark ordeal with Japanese colonialism], initially, the South Koreans welcomed the United States, but

Gen. John Hodge, the head of the U.S. Military Government In South Korea, working under Gen. Douglas MacArthur, quickly brought Koreans who had cooperated with the Japanese during the occupation into the government [an unforgivable offense to the vast majority of the Korean people] and shut out Koreans seeking democracy. He refused to meet with representatives of the KPR and banned the party, working instead with the right wing Korean Democratic Party - made up of landlords, land owners, business interests and pro-Japanese collaborators. Shut out of politics, Koreans who sought an independent democratic state took to other methods and a mass uprising occurred. A strike against the railroads in September 1946 by 8,000 railway workers in Pusan quickly grew into a general strike of workers and students in all of the South's major cities. The US Military Government arrested strike leaders en masse. In Taegu, on Oct. 1, huge riots occurred after the Korean police [still loyal to Japan, as well as to the U.S.] smashed picket lines and fired into a crowd of student demonstrators, killing three and wounding scores. In Yongchon, on Oct. 3, 10,000 people attacked the police station and killed more than 40 police, including the county chief. Some 20 landlords and pro-Japanese officials were also killed. A few days later, the US military declared martial law and effectively crushed the uprising. They fired into large crowds of demonstrators in numerous cities and towns, killing and wounding an unknown number of people.

Syngman Rhee, an exile who had lived in the US for 40 years, was rushed to Tokyo and then to Seoul on MacArthur's personal plane. He initially allied with left leaders to form a government approved of by the U.S. Then in 1947, he dispensed with his left allies by assassinating their leaders. On Jeju Island, the largest Korean island lying in a strategic location in the Korea Strait, there continued to be protests against the US Military Government. It was one of the last areas [in the South] where people's committees continued to exist. Gen. Hodge told Congress Jeju was "a truly communal area that is peacefully controlled by the People's Committee," but, nonetheless, he organized its extermination in a scorched-earth attack.

In September, Rhee's new government launched a massive counterinsurgency operation under US command. Author, Air Force officer during the Vietnam War, lawyer, peace activist, world traveler for investigative journalism, including to both North and South Korea, S. Brian Willson reports [as does Cumings' book] in an article of 6-21-2012 on his website that it resulted in the killing of 60,000 Islanders, with another 40,000 desperately fleeing in boats to Japan. One-third of its residents were either murdered or fled during the extermination campaign. Nearly 40,000 homes were destroyed and 270 of 400 villages were leveled. . . . A quarter of the Jeju population had been massacred. The US embassy happily reported: "The all-out guerilla extermination campaign came to a virtual end in April with order restored and most rebels and sympathizers killed, captured, or converted." [If readers hear echoes of the U.S. anti-insurgency campaigns in the Philippines after "liberating" its people from Spain, their hearing is working perfectly.] More brutality occurred on mainland Korea. On October 19, dissident soldiers in the port city of Yosu rose up in opposition to the war on Jeju. About 2,000 insurgent soldiers took control of the city. By Oct. 20, a number of nearby towns had also been liberated and the People's Committee was reinstated as the governing body. People's courts were established to try police officers, landlords, regime officials and other supporters of the Rhee dictatorship. This rebellion was effectively suppressed by a bloodletting, planned and directed by the US military. The Korean War followed.

The official story of the U.S. government and mainstream education has, since that time, simply been that, in a "legally" divided country, the North attacked the South and, thus, started the war and, thus, they were the bad guys---end of discussion. Émile Meklin, writing on the website Quora, explains in capsule what also is largely captured in Cumings' book:

The DPRK [North Korea] was the first to launch a full scale invasion. However, they weren't the first to attack, necessarily. The years prior to the breakout of war were plagued by border skirmishes, commando raids, etc., usually instigated by the South [even according to U.S. officials]. Thousands of casualties had resulted from these by the time the North launched a full invasion [on June 25th, 1950] which was officially launched in response to the South seizing a disputed border village (something on which

Southern newspapers proudly reported); however the North had been ready to pull the trigger for weeks at that point.

And why not? The Korean Peninsula had been one country for a millennium. And now, after suffering under the yoke of Japanese colonialism for decades, they are being artificially divided, with savage attacks upon the people of the southern half of their country. Who is supposed to intervene? Who is going to go to their defense if not their northern half? Meklin continues:

By the time the North had invaded, hundreds of thousands of "dissidents" had been imprisoned in the South. Once news of the [North's] crossing of the DMZ had reached Seoul, the Rhee government executed many of those imprisoned, viewing them as "potential collaborators," . . . leaving up to 200,000 dead. Some 400,000 citizens were drafted (very much forcibly) into the South's new Republic of Korea Army [ROKA].

In the end, upward of 100,000 Koreans in the southern part were killed in political violence *before* the Korean War [emphasis in original]; once the war began at least another 100,000 were killed [besides the executed prisoners].

S. Brian Willson summarizes the war:

The Korean War, which lasted from June 1950 to July 1953, was an enlargement of the 1948-50 struggle of Jeju Islanders to preserve their self-determination from the tyrannical [and virulently anti-communist] rule of US-supported Rhee and his tiny cadre of wealthy constituents. . . . The War destroyed by U.S. bombing [including incendiary bombs and oceans of napalm] most cities and villages in Korea north of the 38th Parallel [as well as incinerating the North's industrial base] and many south of it . . . while killing five million people [estimates vary, but all acknowledge several million dead, including 37,000 American soldiers with 92,000 wounded] and permanently separating ten million Korean families. Much of this was because the North had little or no air defenses until later in the war. Bragging about the massacre, USAF Strategic Air Command head General Curtis LeMay, summed it up: "Over a period of three years or so we killed off - what - twenty percent of the population." Willson corrects LeMay, writing that it is now believed that the population north of the imposed 38th Parallel lost nearly a third of its population of 8-9 million people during the 37-month war.

Events show the vast majority of the Korean people, in 1945, with the shackles of Japanese rule in ruins, were determined to be independent and were ready to fight any force that would attempt to subjugate them again. In 1945, that turned out to be the United States. The U.S. was attempting to expand and tighten its own grip and the grip of Western global capitalism on the riches of Asia as part of the booty from winning WWII, while also trying to prevent the Korean people's hopes for socialism from becoming a reality. As such, the U.S. was the aggressor in the war and the only unjustified combatant. (Technically, the foreign troops in South Korea were UN troops, but the U.S. provided 90% of them and commanded them.)

The Soviet Union moved into northern Korea (as well as into Manchuria, the northeastern area of China) both because Japan was its enemy, too, and as part of its agreement with the U.S. to join the war against Japan after the defeat of Germany. It provided arms and advisors to the cause of the North, but no troops. Chinese forces entered the war as U.S. forces and their South Korean army, after recovering from their initial setback by the North's push into the South, came back and crossed the 38th parallel, and kept going north, heading straight toward the border of China.

Listen to M. Preston Goodfellow, a regular emissary of the Truman administration to Rhee in Seoul, after returning from Seoul in December, 1949. He was asked how great was the danger of war breaking out in Korea. As recounted in Cumings' book, Goodfellow said:

[I]t was Rhee and the South Koreans anxious to go into N.K. [but the U.S. wouldn't yet give them the green light]. . . . The U.S. Govt. position is this: avoid any initiative on S. Korea's part in attacking N.K., but if N.K. should invade S.K. then S.K. should resist and march right into N.K. with World War III as the result but in such a case, the aggression came

from N.K. and the American people would "understand" [my quotation marks] (145).

The US, pushed back by the Chinese reinforcements, of whom, according to several sources, as many as a million died, the two sides stalemated back at the 38th parallel, where they are still today.

In its rabid compulsion to wipe out their independent will and make them submit, the U.S. massacre of the people of Korea (and China) still stands as an unrecognized international crime of immense magnitude and makes them also responsible for today's continuing strife on the forcibly-divided Korean Peninsula. All of which proves once again how far international capitalism will go to secure for itself greater wealth and control.

Of course, they had already set the bar very high for how far they'll go only five years earlier with the dropping of the atomic bomb on Japan, certainly the single-day record for the most barbarous atrocity ever perpetrated---matched only by the second one they dropped three days later. In the subsequent conventional bombing of Korea, they could easily get under that bar and, thus, had to feel they had a ticket to ride in bombing the North almost to extinction.

As to why they dropped the atomic bomb, heavily questioned even at the time, current "conventional wisdom" was handed down to us by Secretary of War

Henry Stimson. Stimson asserted that using the atomic bomb saved a "million American lives" by making an invasion of Japan unnecessary. As Kai Bird, historian and Pulitzer Prize winning author, writes in an October 15th, 1994 newspaper article:

The million-casualty figure was first used by Secretary of War Henry Stimson in a 1946 Harper's article, but without any supporting evidence. According to the historian James Hershberg, the figure "instantly became the orthodox defense for bombing Hiroshima and Nagasaki."

J. Samuel Walker, the chief historian for the U.S. Regulatory Commission, has written, "The consensus is that the bomb was not needed to avoid an invasion of Japan. It is clear that alternatives to the bomb existed and that Truman and his advisers knew it. The hoary claim that the bomb prevented 500,000 American combat deaths is unsupportable."

According to Stephen E. Ambrose, author of a much-lauded Dwight D. Eisenhower biography, the Allied commander told Secretary Stimson of his "belief that Japan was already defeated and that dropping the bomb was completely unnecessary."

Truman's diary, released in 1979, shows that he knew from decoded Japanese cables that the enemy was about to surrender unconditionally. The only barrier was Tokyo's request for an assurance that the monarchy be retained.

It would seem then that Truman realized the war would end long before the United States could mount an invasion of the Japanese home islands, the first phase of which was not scheduled until Nov. 1.

Their most likely reason for dropping the bomb was indicated by Secretary of State James F. Byrnes who, as author Bird reports in his article, "told the physicist Leo Szilard, 'rattling the bomb might make Russia more manageable.'"

For this hope, the U.S. almost instantly wiped out about 175,000 (conservatively speaking) of a defeated and defenseless population (including from 10,000 to 20,000 Koreans, most of whom had been transported to Japan as cheap laborers during Japan's occupation). A picture of a happy, smiling Truman, upon learning of the "success" of the bomb, is sickeningly revealing. And how did that work out? In 1949, the Soviets exploded their own atomic bomb. The Cold War arms race of MAD---Mutually Assured Destruction---was on. The world has lived under this nuclear threat ever since.

Of course, we are taught that, in any event, the Japanese deserved the atomic bombings because they bombed Pearl Harbor in an "unprovoked, surprise" attack four years earlier, killing 2,400 naval personnel and civilians (as if the destruction of Tokyo in what is considered the most devastating conventional bombing in history, using incendiary, white phosphorous, and napalm bombs, killing 100,000 people near the very end of the war, wouldn't have already quenched their thirst for revenge).

But, while there is much solidly documented evidence that the Pearl Harbor attack was neither unprovoked nor a surprise to the top echelon of the U.S. government and military command, the main point is that this war was a classic example of top global capitalist conflicts. Japan sought colonial conquest in East and Southeast Asia to secure for itself the critical resources it lacked: iron ore and most other essential minerals, and especially oil. However, as in every other area of the world, the Far East was already the colonial province of the established powers. When, for instance, Japan invaded French Indochina in 1940 (including Vietnam), it was not well received since it already "belonged" to France. When Japan invaded China in 1937, it was not tolerated because China had been an enforced, unofficial Western colony for the prior 100 years. (Britain had successfully made two wars on China in the 19th century, joined by France for the second one, to force China to allow "free trade" entry for Britain's lucrative opium exports.)

In other words, there weren't any "good guys." Neither the U.S. nor Japan was engaged in a struggle over how to best serve the interests of the people of Asia. They both wanted to exploit them and their soil. But the U.S. held the cards because the U.S. had been the main source of the resources Japan so sorely needed. For Japan's transgressions, the U.S., along with Britain, imposed a crippling, complete embargo on all trade with them. Japan either had to give up its imperial ambitions or engage the U.S. in war, which evidence says was exactly what the U.S. expected, wanted, and planned for to serve as a pretext to gain the support of the U.S. population to enter World War II. (The American people, according to polls at the time, were very "isolationist" and had no desire to get involved in what was a European war that had already raged for two years.)

As Robert B. Stinnett reports in his book (noted below), hundreds of thousands of papers released through the Freedom of Information Act document that "[D]eliberate steps were planned and implemented to elicit the overt action [by Japan] that catapulted America into the war." And that, on November 27 and 28, 1941 (the attack on Pearl Harbor was on Dec. 7th of that year), US military commanders were given this order: "The United States desires that Japan commit the first overt act." (But the military commanders in Hawaii didn't know the "overt act" was coming their way.) Japan fatefully chose war over surrendering to the embargo and the attack on Pearl Harbor followed.

Many documents have been released over time that confirm what was already widely contended: the U.S. had indeed broken the Japanese code and secretly tracked the Japanese fleet headed toward the U.S. naval base in Hawaii. And that means the U.S. let those 2,400 sailors and civilians go to their deaths in order to establish a pretext they hoped would unite the country behind a declaration of war. (The three aircraft carriers stationed at Pearl Harbor were out on the high seas on "maneuvers" at the time of Japan's attack.) Actually, no one should be very shocked since the U.S. has concocted a public relations pretext for almost every war it's ever waged. (The account relying on the most recent documentation is found in the book, *Day of Deceit: The Truth about FDR and Pearl Harbor*, 2000, by Robert B. Stinnett. Stinnett, by the way, *supports* these calculated and provocative maneuvers leading up to Pearl Harbor, and the U.S. declaration of war, in the interest, as he puts it, of a bigger U.S. role in the "fight for freedom.")

In 1965, Henry Cabot Lodge (formerly U.S. Ambassador to South Vietnam) spoke in Cambridge,

Massachusetts. According to the Boston *Sunday Globe* (February 28, 1965) this is what he said:

> "Geographically, Vietnam stands at the hub of a vast area of the world---Southeast Asia---an area with a vast population of 249 million persons. . . . He who holds or has influence in Vietnam can affect the future of the Philippines and Formosa [Taiwan] to the East, Thailand and Burma with their huge rice surpluses to the West, and Malaysia and Indonesia with their rubber, ore and tin to the South. . . . Vietnam thus does not exist in a geographical vacuum---from it, large store-houses of wealth and population can be influenced and undermined" (*Enemy*, 108).

That brief analysis from one who should know was for those who never answered the oft-asked question during the Vietnam War, even raised in song: "What the hell are we fighting for?" And, not only were they fighting for that described above, they were, at the same time, as they were in Korea and the Philippines, fighting *against* the clearly demonstrated will of the indigenous population, dropping more tons of bombs on the country, North *and* South, than were dropped in all of WWII by all combatants combined.

From *Wall Street's Think Tank*, Laurence H. Shoup, 2015:

> Augusto Pinochet's dictatorship in Chile was the first large-scale implementation of "neoliberalism" [not really something new, it refers to unlimited privatization and

unrestricted capital flow and accumulation]. In September of 1973, socialist Salvador Allende's democratically elected government was overthrown [and General Pinochet installed], followed by a one-sided civil war against the left, with estimates of over 3,000 activists known to have been murdered, over 30,000 tortured, over 80,000 arrested, and millions of people terrorized. Varied people's movements were destroyed and a path opened to unopposed privatization, union destruction, cuts in social spending, deregulation, and so-called free markets.

The U.S. government had sought and organized such a coup since September 15, 1970, when President Richard M. Nixon . . . ordered CIA director . . . Richard Helms to foster a government overthrow in Chile. . . . National Security Adviser Henry A. Kissinger and his assistant Alexander Haig discussed promoting a coup on October 15, 1970. The next day, the CIA station chief in Santiago, Chile received Kissinger's orders via CIA headquarters: "It is firm and continuing policy that Allende be overthrown by a coup. . . . It is imperative that these actions be implemented clandestinely and securely so that the U.S. Government and American hand be well hidden. . . . This imposes upon us a high degree of selectivity in making military contacts." The U.S. ambassador to Chile at the time was Edward M. Korry. Illustrative of the hostility with which the U.S. capitalist class viewed Allende's free election as president of Chile is what Korry said when he heard that Allende had won: "Not a nut or bolt shall reach Chile under Allende. Once Allende comes to power we shall do all within our power to condemn Chile and all Chileans to utmost deprivation and poverty."

Once in power [due to the coup] and his violent system of terror was in place, Dictator Pinochet brought in a group of Chilean economists who had studied with Milton Friedman at the University of Chicago. They implemented a full neoliberal program in Chile, including privatizing many sectors of the economy and society, including public utilities, health care, parts of the education system, and pensions; dramatically cut government social services; and opened the nation to "free" trade. The results of the program: unemployment reached 33 percent in 1982 and by 1988 almost half of Chileans were living in poverty, while the income of the richest 10 percent had increased by 83 percent. Under Pinochet and neoliberalism, Chile had become one of the most unequal nations in the world. The Chilean people eventually rebelled and at great sacrifice ousted the military dictatorship.

From Thomas Friedman, author and long-time star *NY Times* columnist:

"The hidden hand of the market will never work without a hidden fist. McDonald's [fast-food chain] cannot flourish without McDonnell Douglas, the designers of the U.S. Air Force F15" (168-170, 185).

IRAQ

From *The Fire This Time*, Ramsey Clark (former U.S. Attorney General), 1992:

One of the so-called benefits of the destruction of Iraq [during the first U.S. invasion, 1991] was proclaimed in front-page stories across the country some months after the bombing ceased. "Gulf War Gives Boost to U.S. Self Confidence," one story announced, "Americans Have New Faith in Themselves." A former State Department official now employed by the Rand Corporation was heard to say the war gave "a boost to the whole idea of competence."

The moral impoverishment of finding human benefit from such appalling human carnage cannot be laid at the feet of leadership alone. The people, deprived of historical knowledge, contemporary fact, democratic power, and political wisdom, victimized by a culture that glorifies violence and worships Mammon [riches], accept the equation. Therein lies the problem. Presidential popularity reached new heights in the polls after vicious assaults on Grenada, Libya, Panama, and Iraq. People wear "Just Cause" t-shirts with a racist pineapple-face portraying Noriega after the mindless bashing of a small neighbor. Orwell's doublespeak has become the official language of the Pentagon. The media was more adept and equally committed to the doublespeak and glorification of the war. It was largely responsible for the mauling of truth that enabled the American people to celebrate a slaughter and make heroes of those who ordered and committed it.

According to a *New York Times* story on March 8, 1992, the Pentagon dream for U.S. world dominion is set forth in a 46-page document asserting that "America's political and military mission in the post-cold war era will be to insure that no rival superpower is allowed to emerge in Western Europe, Asia, or territory of the former Soviet Union."

It refers to the U.S. destruction of Iraq as a "defining event in U.S. global leadership," and says the "overall objective is to remain the predominant outside power in the region [Middle East] and preserve U.S. and Western access to the region's oil," concluding "we must continue to play a strong role through enhanced deterrence and improved cooperative security."

It states: "[W]e will retain the pre-eminent responsibility for addressing selectively those wrongs which threaten not only our interests, but those of our allies or friends, or which could seriously unsettle international relations." It continues: "Various types of interests may be involved in such instances: access to vital raw materials, primarily Persian Gulf oil."

The overall purpose is summarized by the *Times* as "a world dominated by one superpower whose position can be perpetuated by constructive behavior and sufficient military might to deter any nation or group of nations from challenging American primacy."

The Trident II nuclear submarine, which is on no nuclear arms reduction list, is a weapon beyond imagination. It can launch 24 missiles while submerged. Each missile can contain up to 17 independently targeted, maneuverable nuclear warheads. Each warhead, 10 times more powerful than the bomb that destroyed Nagasaki, can travel up to 7,000 nautical miles and strike within 300 feet of the target. Four hundred and eight cities in Europe or Japan could be hit by nuclear warheads from a single launch. Twenty of these submarines were commissioned, and after the dissolution of the Soviet Union . . . the United States continues to complete the Trident II fleet (219-220, 222-224).

From *Wall Street's Think Tank*:

No more than six weeks after the *second* U.S. invasion of Iraq, in 2003, the U.S., through its special envoy and Civil Administrator, L. Paul Bremer, issued a number of economic edicts. . . . [Two of] Bremer's major orders were:

Order 39: rewriting foreign investment laws in favor of foreign multinational corporations, allowing 100 percent foreign ownership except in the oil sector, privatizing 200 state-owned Iraqi enterprises, and allowing unrestricted, tax-free repatriation of profits out of Iraq.

Order 40: allowing foreign banks to purchase up to 50 percent of an Iraqi bank.

Bremer told a special meeting of the World Economic Forum meeting in Jordan that he would "set in motion policies which will have the effect of reallocating people and resources from state enterprises to more productive private firms." He added that these state enterprises were "inefficient" so their privatization was "essential for Iraq's economic recovery." This resulted in mass unemployment, which reached as high as 50-60 percent during the summer of 2003. . . . As [author] Naomi Klein summed it up:

"[T]he country was transformed into a cut-throat capitalist laboratory---a system that pitted individuals and communities against each other, that eliminated hundreds of thousands of jobs and livelihoods and that replaced the quest for justice with rampant impunity for foreign occupiers."

To defend the neoliberal free market model and attempt to salvage American hegemonic goals, during the first three and a half years of the occupation, an estimated 61,500 Iraqis were captured and imprisoned by U.S. forces, and many were tortured.

Many in the capitalist think tank world have an attitude . . . that is exemplified by Stephanie Sanok who works at the . . . Center for Strategic and International Studies: "We are still sinking a lot of money into this and we are still trying to get our oil dividend."

These capitalists certainly do not want to give up their "oil dividend.". . . They ignore the immorality and lack of elemental ethics and humanity imposed by a catastrophic and criminal war, with the massive destruction, displacement, kidnapping, torture, and murder visited upon the Iraqi people. Though estimates vary, the respected British medical journal *The Lancet* conducted a study and estimated that about 650,000 Iraqis were killed; an unknown, but vast number wounded; and millions displaced from their homes. Almost 8,000 U.S. citizens were killed (almost 4,500 service personnel and at least 3,400 contractors) and over 100,000 wounded. To speak of the lack of an "oil dividend" in light of such an ocean of human suffering is telling (219-221, 233-34).

One can only be open-mouthed and speechless when the U.S. accuses some *other* country (say, Iran) of being a "destabilizing" force in the Middle East!

ON CHINA

From *Wall Street's Think Tank*:

The East and South China Seas are seen as both economic and strategic zones by a number of states---most prominently China, Japan, the Philippines, Vietnam, and the United States---with fish, potential oil and gas resources, tourism, guano, and strategic position (coastal defense, large trade flows, and safe passage to the open Pacific Ocean) all at stake.

For decades the United States has been the dominant naval and military power in the region and at least since 1992 has had the strategic objective of preventing the emergence of a rival superpower. Furthermore, it is now "pivoting" to Asia; for example, beginning to station military forces in northern Australia. . . . China is rapidly ramping up its military spending and military forces. . . . This spending resulted in the launching of China's first aircraft carrier in 2012, with another carrier currently under construction (49).

Is there any question that capitalism, besides being infamous for its criminal and brutal "smaller" wars on poor and weak countries, inevitably, sooner or later, beats a path to BIG war among the major capitalist rivals themselves? (And, when elephants fight, it's the grass beneath their feet that gets trampled.) Further, there can't be any question that China has been thoroughly capitalist for decades, regardless of its labels and state structures that are holdovers from its history as a socialist country almost 45 years ago.

As *Business Insider* reported in its Oct. 10, 2015 issue:

China has gone from being a country that opposed capitalism to one that embraces property rights, profits, and free market competition. . . . [I]n 2015, the Shanghai Stock Exchange is the third-largest in the world by market capitalization. . . . China has entered into a number of regional and bilateral trade agreements, or is in the process of doing so. It currently has free trade agreements with the Association of Southeast Asian Nations (ASEAN), Chile, Costa Rica, Hong Kong, Iceland, Macau, New Zealand, Pakistan, Peru, Singapore and Switzerland. . . . Global institutions, including the International Monetary Fund and World Bank, have endorsed a new China-led international bank, the Asian Infrastructure Investment Bank (AIIB). . . . China hopes to see its currency, the renminbi, become a world-class reserve currency to compete with the U.S. dollar.

And from the Cato Institute's *Policy Report* of Jan, 15, 2013:

The Party has distanced itself from radical ideology; it is no longer communist except in name. China basically became a market economy by the end of the 90s before it joined the World Trade Organization in 2001. In the new millennium, the Chinese economy has . . . become more integrated with the global economy.

According to a World Investment Report of 2007, China was the largest single recipient of foreign direct investments in the developing world from 1992 on. And an Associated Press article of February, 2019 announced that China now has the most billionaires of any country in the world.

There are those who gloatingly point to China's stunning rise as a capitalist economic world power as proof that capitalism is the "best" system. But a closer look at its history tells a different story. Only nine years after the 1949 victory of the socialist revolution led by Mao Tse-tung (a victory the U.S. and Britain were not in a position to prevent due to the circumstances of World War II) China was immersed in industrialization as part of rectifying the inhuman conditions it had been chained to by foreign domination for a very long time. The following is from Felix Greene's 1961, *Awakened China*:

The pace of China's industrial development has outstripped all anticipations and is unprecedented in history. Dr. Charles Bettelheim of the Sorbonne, who was one of a group of French economists who visited China in 1958, reported: "Above all, the feeling prevailing with my economist colleagues and myself is that of finding ourselves in a country that goes ahead at an unbelievable speed and which, in this respect, outdoes all the performances that could have been achieved elsewhere.". . . China's advance in absolute terms is indicated by the fact that in production of coal she is now the second largest producer in the world; in machine tools she has surpassed Britain and Germany; in iron and steel she will quite soon be surpassing all but the United States and the Soviet Union. In cotton production she has already surpassed the United States. In textiles the city of Shanghai alone is out-producing Britain. In September 1958, British experts who keep close touch with developments in China stated that: "The pace of expansion is now such that within less than a decade China should become the third leading industrial power in the world, ranking only after the United States and Russia" (101-103).

Clearly, China's socialism had unleashed the pent up energy of the broad masses and had *already* created a strong economic base and was only beginning. Those occupying high positions in the Communist Party who longed for power and riches bided their time. When Mao died in 1976, they struck immediately (still disguised in their Mao jackets), seizing the reins of power and steering the burgeoning economy onto the capitalist road under the slogan, "To get rich is glorious." (Mao warned of this before his death.) The U.S. was so deliriously happy about China's restoration of capitalism that Time Magazine put Deng Xiaoping, the leader of this coup, on its cover in 1978 as its Man of the Year, and the next year the White House brought him in for a state visit with full military honors. In that same year, the U.S. bestowed most-favored-nation trading status on China. But, in a classic case of "be careful what you wish for," China is now everywhere beating the top capitalist powers at their own "game." The howls and accusations of "unfair practices," and "breaking all the rules," and "we must unite against them," are gathering steam.

We return to the year 1958 to get a deeper sense of the significance and the stakes surrounding China's development as a socialist country. At that time, the U.S. had a travel ban on citizens going to China, including reporters, but that didn't stop some from getting there (including Felix Greene, twice) along with travelers from other countries. More from *Awakened China*:

Reports trickling in from British and Canadian travelers, the accounts given by responsible international scientists of the tremendous advances made in Chinese science and industry have made it impossible to conceal that some very rapid and striking advances have indeed taken place there. These advances have been "explained" in the American press by what one might call the "slave-labor" theory. Thus, there is a prevailing opinion in America that the Chinese are being threatened, brainwashed, or bludgeoned into this work of national industrialization; that a small group of power-hungry Communist leaders have fastened themselves onto an unwilling and resentful population and are driving them fiercely forward against their will (107, 145).

And how would one come by this "prevailing opinion"?

In November, 1958, Secretary of State John Foster Dulles informed an assemblage of nations that the Chinese were "imposing mass slavery on 650 million people." They had "degraded the dignity of the human individual." They had created "a vast slave state."

Scripps-Howard newspapers featured a series of articles entitled "Chain Gang Empire." One of the cartoons illuminating this series offered a row of skulls above a blood-spattered wall, upon which was written (in words of blood) "Family destruction," "bestiality," "slave labor." And Life magazine presented artists' drawings of burning villages and weeping women. [And, also from Life, January, 1959]:

Two Chinese who escaped tell of Reds' harsh regimentation which tears families apart, puts children in barracks, even regulates sex. All over China the family-centered, individualistic Chinese are being reduced to 653 million indistinguishable and interchangeable parts in a vast, inhuman machine.

And, according to an article in the *Christian Science Monitor*, December, 1958, China's technological and industrial advances have been achieved by "the greatest mass sacrifice of human heritage, human comfort, and human effort in all time."

When you have as bloody a track record in stomping out attempts at socialism as the U.S. and its allies do, "merely" broadcasting ghastly lies about it is tame work for them. But, to be "fair," the speakers and authors of the above statements represent capitalism, and capitalism has no genetic code for comprehending the concept of people being motivated to work selflessly for the betterment of all. So, these speakers and writers just might actually have believed that all the Chinese were hypnotized and enslaved because it was the only explanation they could come up with. In any case, they were determined that that would be the explanation the people of the U.S. would embrace. (They told us similar rabid lies about the Russian Revolution and its subsequent socialist society, as well.)

This from the President of the Royal Bank of Canada on his return from China, reporting to his shareholders in the *Royal Bank Magazine*, October, 1958:

> The growth in industry, the change in living standards, the modernization of everything and anything, the feats of human effort and colossal impact of human labor are not within our power to describe and still give a worthwhile picture of the scene. All I can say is that it must be seen to be believed. It is truly stupendous. . . . We think the vast majority of the people of China have a government they want, a government which is improving their lot, a government in which they have confidence, a government which stands no chance of being supplanted.

From an Oxford author of books on physics, discussing the impact of technology on the Chinese people on his return from China, published in *The Listener*, February 1961:

> One of the many slogans which has caught on particularly well is "Learn while you work." . . . I was told that, at the building of the great Yangtze Bridge, they started with a fairly small number of skilled crews. The others watched. Soon

many more could do the skilled work, and so it went on in a chain reaction of learning. . . . The workers of China have this immense desire to learn because they enjoy it and not just because they want better jobs. In terms of industrial production this means that the Chinese scientists and engineers will be backed by a good supply of eager and enthusiastic technicians, a grade in which our own industry is lamentably short.

From an article in *Le Monde*, Paris, October, 1958 by a Professor of Comparative Agriculture at the Agronomic Institute, entitled "Chinese Agriculture":

Without the active and voluntary participation of the majority, the mountains would not have been terraced nor would the terraces have been held in place by gravel, nor would the gravel have been humped, basket by basket, from the river beds. It is my impression that the Chinese Party has succeeded in marrying its authority to the peasant's consent after due deliberation, a consent obtained by protracted explanations.

From a leading lawyer in Ontario, Canada in *Maclean's Magazine*, November 1958:

Having visited such communities this year---and having entered many a peasant home forty years ago---I am amused by the story, zealously spread by certain writers from their posts in Hong Kong and Formosa [Taiwan], that the peasants (five hundred million of them) are kept in the co-ops by coercion and terror.

From an article by Field Marshal Viscount Montgomery in *The Sunday Times*, London, June 1960:

One hears it said that children in the Communes are removed from their parents. I investigated this and found it to be totally untrue. There are great misconceptions in the Western world about this new China, particularly in the United States . . . and that cannot be stated too clearly.

From an article by a historian at Cambridge University, in the *New Statesman*, London, December 1958:

I traveled some 12,000 miles within the country . . . meeting hundreds not only of scientists and scholars but all sorts and conditions of men. My most outstanding impression of China this year was of the unreality of ideas so cherished in the West that the population is dragooned to perform its tasks. On the contrary, everywhere one sees spontaneity (sometimes overrunning government planning), enthusiasm for increasing production and modernization, pride in an ancient culture equipping itself to take its rightful place in the modern world. What has been done in public health, social services, industrial development, and advancing amenities of all kinds and what one sees going on under one's own eyes would be absolutely impossible without the willing and convinced cooperation of all types of workers, manual and intellectual.

And from Felix Greene---author, documentary filmmaker, lecturer, and former senior official of the British Broadcasting Corporation:

While in Peking I had access to the ambassadors and staffs of most of the Western neutral embassies. I also had discussions with many well-informed Europeans who have lived in China for many years. Their reports on the present leadership in China were impressively similar in substance. China is not being led by a group of men hungry for personal power who have fastened themselves on a resentful population. It is, rather, a leadership that has shown itself genuinely concerned with the welfare of the people.

I have come to believe that Mao Tse-tung is not surrounded by yes-men fearful of arousing his displeasure. We are not dealing with a Hitler or Mussolini, or a latter-day Stalin whose moral judgments were poisoned by a paranoid mistrust of those around him. China is being led by historically conscious, strong, and enormously competent men who as far back as the 1920's identified themselves with the people and knew their needs. They won their revolution because they carried out the demands of a people driven to extremities of suffering, and who were determined to end the disease, hunger, and corruption which had held them in subjugation for centuries. If ever in history there was a people's revolution, this was it (*Awakened China*, 148-149).

We have included these few testimonials, not only to expose the gross lies, but to highlight the huge loss caused by the betrayal of this rare and most authentic example ever of revolutionary socialism in action. Beginning in the 1980's with their new "market economy," the betrayers turned China into one of the world's biggest sweatshops and, in the process, snuffed out what was the greatest beacon of inspiration and optimism, not only for the Chinese people, but that literally billions of the most oppressed people of Asia, Africa, and Latin America had demonstrably shared. Now, and for the last 45 years, China has inspired no one except some billionaires hoping to become multi-billionaires.

Returning to the currently intensifying inter-capitalist competition, the particular method the Chinese state employs to direct their domestic society is something the U.S. and its allies just pretend to care about. If the Chinese government is strict and authoritarian, or worse, this just describes, and has always described, many of the U.S.' best friends. The pertinent questions for the U.S. concern the world strength of the Chinese economy and military and its threat as a competitor. Even a casual observer of the last couple of decades cannot doubt that its economy is both deeply inter-dependent with and, at the same time, in intense competition with, the economies of the U.S., Western Europe, and

Japan, all of them seeking to take control, or to keep control, of every part of the world economic market, each of them making self-interested alliances, and all using similar means for the same ends. This is a decidedly capitalist competition of the first magnitude we're watching, and we've seen it before lead directly to all-out world slaughter, in which case any and all weapons at their disposal are and will be considered "legitimate." They develop them for just such an occasion. Just the fact that they are all armed to the teeth proves that they know that war and the threat of war is the constant companion of global capitalism.

From an *Associated Press* article of 4-28-15:

When President Barack Obama and Japanese Prime Minister Shinzo Abe meet today, a major subtext of their discussions will be the world leader not in the room: Chinese President Xi Jinping. China's rise underlies both the economic and security discussions that will highlight Abe's state visit to the White House and is at the heart of Obama's so-called U.S. re-balance [militarily] to the Asia-Pacific region.

Before today's meeting, Japanese and U.S. foreign and defense ministers approved revisions to the U.S.-Japan defense guidelines that boost Japan's military capability amid growing Chinese assertiveness in disputed areas in the East and South China Sea claimed by Beijing. The changes, which strengthen Japan's role in missile defense, mine sweeping and ship inspections, are the first revisions in 18 years to the rules that govern U.S.-Japan defense cooperation.

The meeting also comes as attention heightens in the U.S. over a Trans-Pacific Partnership (TPP) trade agreement---a 12-nation deal to "liberalize" commerce around the Pacific Rim. The U.S. and Japan are the biggest participants in the negotiations. [China was not part of it]. . . . Time and again, Obama has pushed for the trade deal in the face of stiff opposition from his liberal base and labor union allies by arguing that without an agreement with Asian countries, China will step into the breach.

"If we don't write the rules, China will write the rules out in that region," Obama said in an interview with the Wall Street Journal. "We will be shut out---American businesses, American agriculture. That will mean a loss of U.S. jobs."

The TPP negotiations also come as China is working to develop an international infrastructure bank for Asia to fill an estimated $8 trillion gap in infrastructure funding for the region over the next decade. Japan and the U.S., leading shareholders of the World Bank and Asian Development Bank, have notably declined to participate, citing concerns over the new bank's "governance standards."

Secretary of State John Kerry said the . . . historic transformation in the post-WWII [military] relationship between Tokyo and Washington . . . recognizes the "evolving risks and dangers both in Asia-Pacific and across the globe."

UKRAINE

From *Wall Street's Think Tank*, 2015:

Since the fall of the USSR in the early 1990s, there has been a drive on the part of the U.S. and Europe . . . to economically and strategically penetrate the former states that were part of the Soviet bloc. The goal is the full integration of these nations into the U.S.-dominated geopolitical [and economic] empire. [Winning the Cold War wasn't an end in itself but rather the beginning of absorbing the booty, however long it takes.] The most important of these countries is Ukraine, due to its size, resources (including shale gas resources), level of development, and geographic position in the heart of Eastern Europe. It lies in a key position for east-west gas transportation, for example. Zbigniew Brzezinski [counselor to President Johnson and then President Carter's National Security Advisor], in his 1997 work, *The Grand Chessboard*, wrote that Ukraine is one of Eurasia's "vital geopolitical pivots," suggesting that both the EU and NATO should expand to include Ukraine within a "reasonable time frame."

In 1994, he and the Center for Strategic and International Studies established an American-Ukrainian Advisory Committee of nineteen members, ten from the United States, including Henry A. Kissinger, along with the CEOs or chairs of major multinational corporations with actual or potential interests in Eastern Europe. . . . They suggested policies to the U.S. government, including U.S. training for Ukrainian military officers as well as promoting free enterprise and privatization programs in Ukraine. Their goals included an eventual "redefinition of Russia" through changes in Ukraine. They also met during the Clinton administration.

Since the 1990s, a prime means to further the aim of bringing Ukraine into the Western orbit has been the funding of "civil society" groups in that nation by the National Endowment for Democracy (NED). . . . NED has put a high priority on funding Ukrainian groups, and NED's president even called the country "the biggest prize." As a result, NED has spent a vast amount funding private groups in Ukraine; in 2013 alone NED spent millions on sixty-five different projects in the country. This was part of a larger U.S. government effort that resulted in $5 billion being spent in Ukraine since 1991. . . . The geopolitical aspect has been the imperialist expansion of NATO to include nations on the borders of Russia.

As the process of enlargement took place during the 1999-2009 period, Moscow complained bitterly, arguing that this process was threatening core Russian national interests. This was especially true in the case of Ukraine, yet the NATO alliance pushed forward. At its summit in April of 2008, the NATO alliance . . . asserted in a statement that eventually both Georgia and Ukraine "will become members of NATO."

In 2013-14, the conflict between the West and Russia over Ukraine's future became more serious, with each side pushing harder to bring Ukraine into its own sphere. The economic stakes were outlined clearly by the U.S. ambassador to Ukraine in a speech of September 3, 2013, when he stated in clear geo-economic language that "Ukraine . . . has the opportunity to become the eastern frontier of a large European economic space at the same time that it serves as Europe's gateway to the Eurasian heartland and Europe's gateway to one of the most dynamic economic regions of the world which stretches all the way to Shanghai and Vladivostok." Both sides offered economic "association" deals designed to tie Ukraine to one of the two competing blocs. When President Viktor Yanukovich chose the Russian counter offer to the negotiated agreement with the EU in November 2013, anti-government demonstrations led to a coup in February of 2014. It is clear that Washington backed the coup, and a State Department official and Senator John S. McCain traveled to Kiev and participated in anti-government demonstrations.

The new government in Kiev was not only pro-Western and anti-Russian, it also included at least four neo-fascists in high-ranking positions. Responses to this right-wing coup included an armed rebellion by local people in the Crimea and eastern Ukraine, clearly encouraged and supported by Russia, including the use of Russian Special Forces. This resulted in a civil war between Kiev and its eastern provinces with dangerous implications for the future of peace in Europe due to the involvement of great powers on each side. Gradually escalating Western-imposed sanctions on Russia was another result. The stakes in this conflict are especially high for Russia, since its people have suffered greatly in the past when several aggressors were able to invade their territory through Ukraine (251-254).

THE PROFOUNDLY CAPITALIST TRAP

The great Latin American writer Eduardo Galeano pointed out that, "In the outskirts of the world [Bangladesh, for example], the system reveals its true face."

Again from *Wall Street's Think Tank*:

The ruthless exploitation of garment workers, the great majority of them women, in Bangladesh is one example of "neoliberalism" [again, unrestricted international capitalism] at work. Bangladesh is an "export powerhouse," with "Made in Bangladesh" labels commonplace in many U.S. and European stores. Bangladesh apparel exports are based on foreign investment, ultra-cheap labor, and an "investment–friendly" government at the service of foreign and domestic bosses. The result is horrible conditions similar to those in the early Industrial Revolution, and Bangladesh has been called the "most dangerous place in the world" for garment workers. Over three and a half million workers work ten to fifteen hours a day, six days a week, for a minimum wage of $37/month (about $1.25/day), in often dangerous working conditions, and severe repression of any attempt to organize the workforce to promote the interests of the rank and file. Special government paramilitary police, called the "Rapid Action Battalion," together with intelligence agencies like the National Police Intelligence Service, closely watch industrial areas and workers who try to organize. Numerous instances of threats, beatings, firings, and black-listings, as well as cases of torture and murder of worker-organizers, amounting to corporate-inspired terrorism, have been documented. . . . Another danger faced by the workers is building collapse or fire in their workplaces, which are often unsafe and have locked doors with no emergency exits. In late November, 2012, a fire in a factory producing clothing for Walmart, Disney, Sears, and others killed 112 workers. In April 2013 at least 1127 workers died in the collapse of an unsafe building. . . . The *New York Times* reported that Walmart, an anti-union corporation, was directly responsible for blocking a 2011 effort to improve fire safety in Bangladesh, its representative arguing that it was not "financially feasible" to do so. This from a corporation owned by a U.S. family whose net worth is over $100 billion (270).

Not defending them---hardly---but, as is probably well understood, Walmart got to where it's at by being "financially feasible," which, under capitalism, means keeping its "overhead" as low as possible. And if it stopped doing so, it would mean improving pay and working conditions and losing profits and, thus, at the same time, raising its prices, losing market share to its competitors and, ultimately, see its stock plummet and possibly face a crisis. Walmart is the perfect example to illustrate that, while capitalism certainly breeds greediness, what we see as human greed is really just the personification of capital, which is in a constant life-and-death battle to expand against the ferocious competition from other blocs of capital bent on swallowing and supplanting it. It isn't individual character flaws that have shaped the world but rather the nature of capitalism itself. Capitalists come and go over generations, but the system of global capitalism grows more and more rapacious and expansionist as each bloc acquires more and more massive holdings in the world. And, still, as it was in the beginning, utterly without a conscience.

From a *Market Watch* stock market research report of Sept., 2012:

The world of large business enterprises is a harsh and fiercely competitive jungle. Any failure to keep your claws sharp enough and your teeth exposed enough may result in finding two sets of those deep in your neck.

While competition can, of course, act as social recreation and entertainment and has a place in every culture, under the rule of big-time capitalism, it does not have a benign purpose. As most people know, the nature of capitalist competition (short of war) is a world-wide, titanic battle primarily in the economic realm. As is also well known, economic competition is first and foremost a "productivity" issue: how much product can be produced with the lowest cost of production, including in the least amount of time, making each commodity as inexpensive as possible. Then they must have a market for those products or they're worthless to the capitalist. Thus, the life-and-death scramble to capture or keep markets for their goods drives the insatiable quest for cheaper and cheaper labor in order to underprice their rivals and seize the markets. (Of course, if and when they seize a near-monopoly, which is their aim, prices often rise.) The place where a capitalist can best control and reduce costs is right at the point of production. Thus, we have the example, above, of the garment workers in Bangladesh. This is, and has been for a long, long time, the broad and constant result of capitalism's vaunted "competitiveness." Of course, the retort in the rich countries is, "But competition keeps prices down." So, two-thirds of humanity should live all their lives in misery and poverty so you can have lower prices? Really? This is a good design for a humane global system?

We have been so inundated with the concept that everything runs better, and maybe will *only* run, with competition, that Walmart's defense that providing more effective protection against factory fires, or raising pay, etc. would make them financially unable to compete is instantly accepted as a legitimate defense. And, under capitalism, *it is*. And, thus, the workers of the world, especially of the southern continents, are caught in a profoundly capitalist trap.

Of course, most of us average people in the U.S. and Western Europe haven't witnessed the reality of the grinding exploitation of the people of the Third World. Examples are rampant throughout the southern continents.

From a 1992 report by an investigative reporter from Nike's home area of Oregon, for the *Newhouse News Service*:

> Over and over throughout the day, Tri Mugiyanti dabs paint on the soles of fresh-off-the-mold Nike sneakers. Around her on the production line, workers sit or stand elbow-to-elbow. . . . The humid air reeks of paints and glues. The temperature hovers near 100 degrees. Breathing feels unnatural.
>
> Welcome to the Hardaya Aneka Shoes Industry factory, known as Hasi, (in Tangerang, Indonesia) on the outskirts of the capital city of Jakarta. Each hour here, 6,700 workers crank out about 2,000 pairs of Nike shoes. . . . For U.S.-based Nike Inc., which has roamed through Asia for 20 years in pursuit of ever-cheaper production sources, Indonesia is the newest frontier.

According to a May, 1993 report printed in the Cleveland *Plain Dealer* newspaper, in the mid-1980s, along with most other shoe companies, Nike escaped the union contracts, pay scale, and regulated working conditions in the U.S., which were infringing on their profits, by shifting its operations to 3rd World countries to keep up with the competition. According to the report, Nike turned first to South Korea, but after workers there won the legal rights to form unions and conduct effective strikes that could raise their pay, the corporation turned elsewhere. Indonesia is notably lax in protecting workers but, just in case, Nike is exploring even more accommodating countries, from Asia to Mexico.

To a great extent, the use of Third World labor fuels Western consumer society and helps pad the wallets of millions of shareholders in U.S.-based marketing companies like Nike. By wringing pennies out of the production process, Nike and other successful consumer products companies fill bags full of money which then arm their big-gun advertising and marketing machines.

Nike will spend $180 million on advertising this year [another obvious expression of the intense competition for market share in which they are locked]. In contrast, it has nothing invested in manufacturing plants or equipment. Instead, the company . . . contracts with 35 independent shoe factories sprinkled like colonies throughout Indonesia, China, Thailand, South Korea, and Taiwan.

The arrangement buoys Nike's gross margin of profit---a hardy 39% for the fiscal year just ended [1992]---and [at the same time] keeps the company at arm's length from the labor-intensive . . . [and incriminatingly brutal] manufacturing business.

Stay 10 minutes in the Hasi factory . . . and your head will pound, your eyes and lips will burn. Amid the glue and paint fumes, workers without protective clothing operate hot molds, presses and cutting machines. A rubber-room fire killed one worker last year.

The factory, which cranks out 370,000 pairs of Nikes a month and aims to do more, must work into the night to keep up with demand. Compulsory overtime is illegal in Indonesia. But enforcement is lax, and Tri and her co-workers would lose their jobs if they refused the additional hours. Besides, it is hard to survive without the extra money.

Tri . . . earns 15 cents an hour. . . . Even in Indonesia, where per-capita income is $585 a year, the wages of shoe factory workers are 35% below the government's standard for the minimum physical needs of a single adult. As in many 3rd World countries, Indonesia's minimum wage is less than poverty level. . . . Because one pilfered pair of Nikes yields the equivalent of a half-month's salary for workers who sell them on the street, security is tight at Hasi. Guards stationed at the factory doorways and gates frisk workers at the end of their shifts.

[The reporter followed Tri home from the factory and reported that] she shares one room in a slum less than a mile from the Hasi factory with three other workers. . . . She sleeps on a bamboo mat. There is no electricity or running water in the shack where Tri lives or in those in which most of the other workers live.

Tangerang has seen rapid industrial development. Factories that make everything from crackers to clothing---mainly for Western markets---pepper the landscape. Neighborhoods of crudely constructed apartments, retail shops and food stands brim with workers chasing a better life and future. They have come to Tangerang from poor villages on the islands of Java and Sumatra. Many, Tri among them, send part of their earnings home to family members. Everything in Tangerang looks temporary, as if a good monsoon would carry away the whole neighborhood.

For Nike, Tangerang is a whistle-stop on the line to cheaper labor.

It should be pointed out that this movement by corporate capitalism that's been going on for several decades to locate their manufacturing in the 3rd World not only serves their voracious need for super-profits but, significantly, it allows them to export the class struggle. That makes it possible to maintain a relatively orderly social and political process in the homeland. Capitalism, by its very nature, means war, but not only war on other countries. It also, from the beginning, has meant class war. There was a time when capitalism regularly bared its fangs to the U.S. working class. As early examples:

During the 1877 railroad strike, started in West Virginia to prevent a third wage cut in a year's time, governors in seven different states called out their militia. By the time government troops, traveling from city to city via trains, finally quelled the uprising after two weeks of effort, over a hundred people had been killed and many more were imprisoned. . . . Between 1877 and 1900, American presidents sent the U.S. Army into eleven strikes, governors mobilized the National Guard in somewhere between 118 and 160 labor disputes, and mayors called out the police on numerous occasions (G.W. Domhoff and Michael J. Webber, *Class and Power in the New Deal*).

This class warfare in the U.S., though often with less violence and with many ups and downs due to both economic and political factors, persisted through WWI, the Great Depression, WWII, and into the 1970s. In terms of numbers, it reached its peak in 1952 when 470 strikes, each involving at least 1000 workers, took place. It can be no coincidence that, beginning in the 1980s, as industrial corporations moved en masse into 3rd World countries, the number of strikes plummeted into comparative nonexistence, and the industrial class struggle, for the next 40 years, up to the present, virtually disappeared. That is, it disappeared within the U.S., only to emerge and take root in the poor and weak countries. And, in its turn, the outlandishly high profits made from cheap labor in the 3rd World have been the source of the higher industrial wages in the home country that have kept relative labor peace. There are countless examples of the intense class struggle with which international capitalism has saddled the people and the societies of the southern hemisphere.

From a Jan., 2014 *New York Times* article:

After months of inaction in the face of growing public dissent to his rule, [Cambodian] Prime Minister Hun Sen appeared to signal that he was entering a more aggressive posture toward his critics. The crackdown came after a clash between protesting garment workers and the Cambodian police that left four of the demonstrators dead. The workers have been at the forefront of growing protests against Mr. Hun Sen's government.

Economic growth that has brought modernity and prosperity to Phnom Penh [the capital] has exposed stark inequalities in the country, where well over a third of children are malnourished. Only one-quarter of the Cambodian population has access to electricity. The Streets of Phnom Penh are shared by luxury cars and families of four squeezed onto dilapidated motorcycles.

Garment workers, who number in the hundreds of thousands, have been the most aggressive in seeking higher wages. Striking workers are demanding a doubling of the monthly minimum wage of $80, an increase that the industry says will make it uncompetitive.

It should be noted that, while little more than 2% of garments now sold in the U.S. are still made here, of those tens of thousands of garment workers remaining in U.S. factories, the great majority are from Asia and Mexico, and many are "illegals." Thus, the workers are inclined to keep quiet about unpaid wages and disregarded safety regulations. While it's still cheaper to manufacture clothes in the 3rd World, these particular clothing corporations can slap a "made in the USA" label on the garments and hope U.S. consumers favor them as being "good" capitalists.

We use the conventional criteria for the definition of a factory "sweatshop": at least two of the following---extremely low wages, extremely long working hours, and serious health and safety risks.

From a *BBC News* report of March, 2016:

Sweatshop conditions resemble prison labor in many cases. In 2014 Apple was caught "failing to protect its workers" in one of its Pegatron [China] factories. Overwhelmed workers were caught falling asleep during their 12-hour shifts and an undercover reporter had to work 18 days in a row. Sweatshops in question carry characteristics such as compulsory pregnancy tests for female laborers and terrorization from supervisors into submission. Workers then go into a state of forced labor; if even one day of work is not accounted for, most are immediately fired. These working conditions have been the source of suicidal unrest within

factories in the past. Chinese sweatshops known to have increased numbers of suicidal employees have suicide nets covering the whole site, in place to stop over-worked and stressed employees from leaping to their deaths.

Sweatshop employees throughout the 3rd World are of the same class of destitute, landless, unemployed peasantry that had already been deliberately created and exploited under the long and brutal rule of colonial capitalism. But, in the post-colonial era, instead of a "mother" country's capitalists having, in many cases, exclusive access to their raw materials and labor power, the newly "independent" countries became fair game for *all* the global predators of "free enterprise." This is what succeeded colonialism when it passed away in the mid-20th century and, because of the intensified competition, as well as new techniques, it brought an *intensification of the exploitation.* By the 1980s, major corporations were contracting with factories throughout the southern hemisphere to "access" that cheap labor force, and it was open season on the workers. Today, locally operating factories stumble over each other, offering to manufacture commodities for less and less, and local state governments vie with each other, competing to win the contracts in a race to the bottom in terms of cheaper and cheaper labor. This is the unspoken essence of modern *globalization.*

From *Open Democracy*, "Harsh Labor: Bedrock of Global Capitalism," March, 2015:

Transnational firms have raised the rate of labor exploitation throughout their supply chains, north and south. Downward pressure on wages and conditions in one part of the chain generates similar pressures elsewhere in the chain, *ad infinitum*. . . . Contemporary global capitalism is predicated upon an enormous and impoverished global laboring class. The mainstream media and development industry portray globalization as a benign sphere of opportunity, and sweatshops as pathways out of poverty. There are numerous grassroots campaigns, by laboring class and non-governmental organizations, as well as by more responsible governments, to combat one aspect or another of harsh labor. However, many of these campaigns understand harsh labor as a consequence of corporate malpractice, rather than as a structural feature of the global economy.

From *Bloomberg News*, Nov., 2006:

Like hundreds of thousands of workers in Latin America, dos Reis collects no wages. He toils six days a week and can't afford to leave; he doesn't have enough money to get back to his home in Teresina, 500 miles (805 kilometers) away in northeastern Brazil. Dos Reis lives next to the brick kilns at Transcameta in a shack with no ventilation, running water, or electricity.

The charcoal he and the other laborers produce by burning scraps of hardwood (in a charcoal-making camp, one of about 1,000 in the Amazon) will be trucked to a blast furnace. . . . It will be used there to make pig iron, a basic ingredient of steel. That pig iron will be purchased by brokers, sold to steelmakers and foundries, and the steel then purchased by some of the world's largest companies for use in cars, tractors, sinks, and refrigerators made for U.S. consumers. [The layers of buyers in this process, all seeking the lowest price possible, result in the gut-wrenching exploitation we see here. In order for this setup to operate, such exploitation at the bottom is *required*.]

"These are people who have absolutely no economic value except as cheap labor under the most inhumane conditions imaginable," says a spokesman for the UN's International Labor Organization (ILO).

Recruiters dispatched by slave-camp owners promise steady-paying jobs, the ILO spokesman says. Once at the Amazon camps, some workers are forced -- at times at gunpoint -- to work off debts to their bosses for food and clothing bought at company stores.

Many go months without pay or see their wages whittled to nothing because of expenses such as tools, boots and gloves. Lack of money, an impenetrable jungle, and a long distance to get home make it impossible for the slaves to leave.

"The truth is that if the government today insisted that the industry here use only 100 percent certifiably legal charcoal, the whole industry . . . would have to shut down," he says.

[N]early 1 million men and women work for little or no wages as forced laborers in Latin America, according to the ILO.

About 25,000 of them work in gold-panning sites in the Amazon, producing more than 7 metric tons a year. There are at least 2,000 such mines stretching for a total length of 125 miles, which have turned rain forest into a moonscape of scarred mounds and rivers choked with mercury-tainted silt.

The gold makes its way into some of the biggest banks in the world, says a general manager at a London-based gold refiner which buys most of the gold from the area. The refiner declined to comment about slavery. . . . A judge based in a town of 12,000 in the Peruvian Amazon says he is investigating more than 30 slavery cases.

Men and women take jobs in slave camps because there's no work to be found at home. [And no land available to them on which to make even a subsistence living. Colonial and neo-colonial capitalism saw to that long ago. The same near-slavery is documented on a large scale in the seafood industry concentrated in Asia.]

From an Oct., 2007 *Bloomberg* report:

Citigroup Inc., IBM Corp., and dozens of other companies must face a $400 billion lawsuit accusing them of aiding South Africa's former apartheid regime. . . . Among the more than 50 defendants in the case are JPMorgan Chase & Co., General Motors Corp., Exxon Mobil Corp., and Credit Suisse Group. Those who sued, including people who were tortured or relatives of those killed, invoked the Alien Tort Claims Act . . . saying the companies knowingly helped the former South African regime by selling it weapons, providing it financing, and otherwise doing business there. . . . The plaintiffs said the companies benefited from South African government policies that provided them with cheap labor, cheap power and high levels of government service. After the United Nations labeled apartheid a ``crime against humanity,'' many companies publicly withdrew from South Africa while maintaining profitable entities there, according to the suit. . . . Until its repeal [in the mid-1990s] the apartheid system denied civil rights to black South Africans, who make up more than 90 percent of the country's 45 million population, forcing them to live in segregated areas and denying them the right to vote. The plaintiffs said that workers were enslaved, tortured, beaten and underpaid during apartheid.

From a June, 1992 *Associated Press* article:

Hundreds of millions of children worldwide toil in fields, factories and even brothels, sacrificing their youth, health, and innocence for pitiful wages, according to a new U.N. report. . . . The most pressing concern is to remove children from the most hazardous work sites, such as glass factories, stone quarries, and garbage dumps, it said.

The report said children who work were far more prone than their peers to have bone deformity, malnutrition, and fatigue. About half the children working in Pakistan's carpet industry die before age 12 because of malnutrition and disease.

An estimated 1 million children in India work in bonded labor in brick kilns, stone quarries and construction, and thousands more in carpet-weaving. If children are paid at all, the wages are usually pitifully low, the report said. Children in light bulb factories in Indonesia work a 48-hour week for about $3 and child coffee-pickers in Zimbabwe earn the same for a 60-hour week, it said. Such wages are less than half the average pay in those countries.

From an October, 2007 *Associated Press* report:

Clothing retailer Gap Inc. said that it will convene all of its Indian suppliers to "forcefully reiterate" its prohibition on child labor after a British newspaper found children as young as 10 making Gap clothes at a sweatshop in New Delhi. Some, working as long as 16 hours a day to hand-sew clothing, said they were not being paid at the unidentified Gap supplier because their employer said they were still trainees. [Even if we're to believe Gap was not aware of child labor practices at its suppliers, Gap certainly was well aware of and had no quarrel with, nor questions about, the ultra-low prices at which it could purchase from such suppliers.] The company also owns Old Navy and Banana Republic and operates more than 3,100 retail stores in the U.S., United Kingdom, Canada, France, Ireland, and Japan.

And, since the corporations can't move their U.S. agricultural fields to the cheap labor in the 3rd World, they move that cheap (and powerless) labor to their fields in the U.S.

From a November, 2007 article in the *New York Times*:

The 10,000 migrant farm workers who harvest tomatoes in South Florida have one of the nation's most backbreaking jobs. For 10 to 12 hours a day, they pick tomatoes by hand. During a typical day, each migrant picks, carries and unloads two tons of tomatoes.

Florida's tomato growers have long faced pressure to reduce operating costs; one way to do that is to keep migrant wages as low as possible. Although some of the pressure has come from increased competition with Mexican growers, most of it has been forcefully applied by the largest purchaser of Florida tomatoes: American fast food chains that want millions of pounds of cheap tomatoes as a garnish for their hamburgers, tacos and salads.

In 2005, Florida tomato pickers gained their first significant pay raise since the late 1970s when Taco Bell ended a consumer boycott by agreeing to pay an extra penny per pound for its tomatoes, with the extra cent going directly to the farm workers. Last April, McDonald's agreed to a similar arrangement. But Burger King has adamantly refused to pay the extra penny — and its refusal has encouraged tomato growers to cancel the deals already struck with Taco Bell and McDonald's.

Migrant farm laborers have long been among America's most impoverished workers. Perhaps 80 percent of the migrants in Florida are illegal immigrants and thus especially vulnerable to abuse. During the past decade, the United States Justice Department has prosecuted half a dozen cases of slavery among farm workers in Florida. Migrants have been driven into debt, forced to work for nothing and kept in chained trailers at night.

Dark Hearts

By George Monbiot, published in the *Guardian*, 24th of April, 2012:

We British have a peculiar ability to blot out our colonial history. There is one thing you can say for the Holocaust deniers: at least they know what they are denying. In order to sustain the lies they tell, they must engage in strenuous falsification. To dismiss Britain's colonial atrocities, no such effort is required. Most people appear to be unaware that anything needs to be denied.

The story of benign imperialism, whose overriding purpose was not to seize land, labour and commodities but to teach the natives English, table manners and double-entry book-keeping, is a myth that has been carefully propagated by the right-wing press. But it draws its power from a remarkable national ability to airbrush and disregard our past.

Last week's revelations that the British government systematically destroyed the documents detailing mistreatment of its colonial subjects, and that the Foreign Office then lied about a secret cache of files containing lesser revelations, is by any standards a big story. But it was either ignored or consigned to a footnote by most of the British press. I was unable to find any mention of the secret archive on the Telegraph's website. The Mail's only coverage, as far as I can determine, was an opinion piece by a historian called Lawrence James, who used the occasion to insist that any deficiencies in the management of the colonies were the work of "a sprinkling of misfits, incompetents and bullies" while everyone else was "dedicated, loyal and disciplined."

The British government's suppression of evidence was scarcely necessary. Even when the documentation of great crimes is abundant, it is not denied but simply ignored. In an article for the Daily Mail in 2010, for example, the historian Dominic Sandbrook announced that "Britain's empire stands out as a beacon of tolerance, decency and the rule of law. . . . Nor did Britain countenance anything like the dreadful tortures committed in French Algeria." Could he really have been unaware of the history he is disavowing?

Caroline Elkins, a professor at Harvard, spent nearly ten years compiling the evidence contained in her book Britain's Gulag: the Brutal End of Empire in Kenya. She started her research with the belief that the British account of the suppression of the Kikuyu's Mau Mau revolt in the 1950s was largely accurate. Then she discovered that most of the documentation had been destroyed. She worked through the remaining archives, then conducted 600 hours of interviews with Kikuyu survivors – both rebels and loyalists – and British guards, settlers and officials. Her book is fully and thoroughly documented. It won the Pulitzer Prize. But as far as Sandbrook, James, and the other imperial apologists are concerned, it might as well never have been written.

Elkins reveals that the British detained not 80,000 Kikuyu, as the official histories maintained, but almost the entire population of one and a half million people, in camps and fortified villages. There, thousands were beaten to death or died from malnutrition, typhoid, tuberculosis and dysentery. In some camps almost all the children died.

The inmates were used as slave labour. Above the gates were edifying slogans, such as "Labour and freedom" and "He who helps himself will also be helped." Loudspeakers broadcast the national anthem and patriotic exhortations. People deemed to have disobeyed the rules were killed in front of the others. The survivors were forced to dig mass graves, which were quickly filled. Unless you have a strong stomach I advise you to skip the next paragraph.

Interrogation under torture was widespread. Many of the men were anally raped, using knives, broken bottles, rifle barrels, snakes and scorpions. A favourite technique was to hold a man upside down, his head in a bucket of water, while sand was rammed into his rectum with a stick. Women were gang-raped by the guards. People were mauled by dogs and electrocuted. The British devised a special tool which they used for first crushing and then ripping off testicles. They used pliers to mutilate women's breasts. They cut off inmates' ears and fingers and gouged out their eyes. They dragged people behind Land Rovers until their bodies disintegrated. Men were rolled up in barbed wire and kicked around the compound.

Elkins provides a wealth of evidence to show that the horrors of the camps were endorsed at the highest levels. The governor of Kenya, Sir Evelyn Baring, regularly intervened to prevent the perpetrators from being brought to justice. The colonial secretary, Alan Lennox-Boyd, repeatedly lied to the House of Commons. This is a vast, systematic crime for which there has been no reckoning.

No matter. Even those who acknowledge that something happened write as if Elkins and her work did not exist. In the Telegraph, Daniel Hannan maintains that just eleven people were beaten to death. Apart from that, "1,090 terrorists were hanged and as many as 71,000 detained without due process."

The British did not do body counts, and most victims were buried in unmarked graves. But it is clear that tens of thousands, possibly hundreds of thousands, of Kikuyu died in the camps and during the round-ups. Hannan's is one of the most blatant examples of revisionism I have ever encountered.

Without explaining what this means, Lawrence James concedes that "harsh measures" were sometimes used, but he maintains that "while the Mau Mau were terrorizing the Kikuyu, veterinary surgeons in the Colonial Service were teaching tribesmen how to deal with cattle plagues." The theft of the Kikuyu's land and livestock, the starvation and killings, the widespread support among the Kikuyu for the Mau Mau's attempt to reclaim their land and freedom: all vanish into thin air. Both men maintain that the British government acted to stop any abuses as soon as they were revealed.

What I find remarkable is not that they write such things, but that these distortions go almost unchallenged. The myths of empire are so well-established that we appear to blot out countervailing stories even as they are told. As evidence from the manufactured Indian famines of the 1870s and from the treatment of other colonies accumulates, British imperialism emerges as no better and in some cases even worse than the imperialism practiced by other nations. Yet the myth of the civilizing mission remains untroubled by the evidence.

On June 7th, 2013, a little over a year after Monbiot's article appeared, we have this tiny article in the Cleveland Plain Dealer to let us know that:

Britain Apologizes To Tortured Kenyans

Britain expressed its "sincere regret" to Kenyans tortured during the Mau Mau uprising in the 1950s and '60s and announced a $31 million compensation package for the victims. Thousands of Kenyans were killed when British and Kenyan allied forces put down the rebellion by the Mau Mau movement, which attempted to end British rule. Others were imprisoned and suffered horrendous abuse, including rape and castration. The compensation money is to be shared among 5,228 victims.

And then we have this little September 14, 2018 Plain Dealer article:

Macron Admits Tortures In Algeria War

France will formally recognize the French military's systemic use of torture in the Algerian War in the 1950s and 1960s, an unprecedented step forward in grappling with its long-suppressed legacy of colonial crimes. President Emmanuel Macron announced his watershed decision in the context of a call for clarity on the fate of Maurice Audin, a Communist mathematician and anti-colonial militant who was tortured by the French army and disappeared in 1957 in the midst of Algeria's bloody struggle for independence from France. Audin's death is a specific case, but it represents a cruel system put in place at the state-level, the Elysée Palace said.

Of course, these crimes by Britain and France, as well as those committed by virtually all colonial powers, were already widely documented and their admissions are only self-serving. They are meant to distance if not entirely disconnect themselves from those crimes as if they are ancient and irrelevant history. But, nonetheless, their confessions highlight and verify how desperately brutal was Europe's reaction to the unstoppable movement for colonial independence after the world-wide slaughter of the 2nd World War was touted to be fought in pursuit of "freedom, democracy, and self-determination."

Mawuna Koutonin, social activist for Africa Renaissance, expands on the description and consequences of those European reactions, citing the French in Africa. This is taken from his January, 2014 article on his website, SiliconAfrica:

When Sékou Touré of Guinea decided in 1958 to get out of the French colonial empire and opted for the country's independence, the French colonial elite in Paris got so furious, and in an historic act of that fury, the French administration in Guinea destroyed everything in the country which represented what they called the benefits from French colonization.

Three thousand French left the country, taking all their property and destroying anything that could not be moved: schools, nurseries, public administration buildings were crumbled; cars, books, medicine, research institute instruments, and tractors were crushed and sabotaged;

horses and cows in the farms were killed, and food in warehouses was burned or poisoned.

It should be noted that much of the property mentioned above was for the use and benefit of the French community living in Africa, including the staff and families of the colonial administration.

The purpose of this outrageous act was to send a clear message to all other colonies that the consequences for rejecting France would be very high.

Sylvanus Olympio, the first president of the Republic of Togo, a tiny country in West Africa, sought a middle ground solution with the French. He didn't want his country to continue to be a French dominion, therefore he refused to sign the colonization continuation pact that [French president Charles] De Gaulle proposed, but agreed to pay an annual debt to France for the so called benefits Togo got from French colonization.

It was the only condition for the French not to destroy the country before leaving. However, the amount estimated by France was so big that the reimbursement of the so-called "colonial debt" was close to 40% of the country's budget in 1963.

The financial situation of the newly independent Togo was very unstable, so in order to get out of the situation, Olympio decided to get out of the French colonial money FCFA (the franc for French African colonies), and issue the country's own currency.

On January 13, 1963, three days after he started printing his country's own currency, a squad of soldiers backed by France killed the first elected president of newly independent Africa. Olympio was killed by an ex-French Foreign Legionnaire army sergeant named Etienne Gnassingbe who supposedly received a bounty of $612 from the local French embassy for the hit man job.

Olympio's dream was to build an independent, self-sufficient, and self-reliant country. But the French didn't like the idea.

On June 30, 1962, Modiba Keita, the first president of the Republic of Mali, decided to withdraw from the French colonial currency FCFA which was imposed on 12 newly independent African countries. For the Malian president, who was leaning more to a socialist economy, it was clear that a colonization continuation pact with France was a trap, a burden for the country's development.

On November 19, 1968, like Olympio, Keita became the victim of a coup carried out by another ex-French Foreign Legionnaire, Lieutenant Moussa Traoré. In fact during that turbulent period of Africans fighting to liberate themselves from European colonization, France would repeatedly use many ex-Foreign Legionnaires to carry out coups against elected presidents:

- On January 1st, 1966, Jean-Bédel Bokassa, an ex-French Foreign Legionnaire, carried out a coup against David Dacko, the first President of the Central African Republic.

- On January 3, 1966, Maurice Yaméogo, the first President of the Republic of Upper Volta, now called Burkina Faso, was the victim of a coup carried out by Aboubacar Sangoulé Lamizana, an ex-French Legionnaire who fought with French troops in Indonesia and Algeria against those countries' independence.

- On 26 October 1972, Mathieu Kérékou, who was a security guard to President Hubert Maga, the first President of the Republic of Benin, carried out a coup against the president after he attended French military schools from 1968 to 1970.

In fact, during the last 50 years, a total of 67 coups happened in 26 countries in Africa, 16 of which are French ex-colonies, which means 61% of the coups happened in Francophone Africa.

This sweeping phenomenon was a direct result of France (like other imperialist powers) making the post-colonial adjustment to losing direct control over its former colonies. The "ex"-colonial masters would still need "reliable" officials in high places in their newly "independent" ex-colonies, and they saw to it.

As these numbers [and events] demonstrate, France is quite desperately keeping a strong hold on its colonies whatever the cost, no matter what. Former French president, François Mitterand, prophesied in 1957 that:

"Without Africa, France will have no history in the 21st century."

In March 2008, former French President Jacques Chirac echoed Mitterand, saying:

"Without Africa, France will slide down into the rank of a third rate power."

At this very moment I'm writing this article, 14 African countries are obliged by France, through a colonial pact, to put 85% of their foreign reserve into France's central bank under French minister of Finance control. Until even now, 2014, Togo and 13 other African countries still have to pay a colonial debt to France. African leaders who refuse are killed or are victims of a coup. Those who obey are supported and rewarded by France with lavish lifestyle while their people endure extreme poverty, and desperation.

We often accuse African leaders of corruption and serving western nations interests, but there is a clear explanation for that behavior. They behave so because they are afraid they'll be killed or a victim of a coup. They want a powerful nation to back them in case of aggression or trouble. But, contrary to a friendly nation's protection, the western protection is often offered in exchange for these leaders renouncing to serve their own people's or nations' interests.

In 1958, scared about the consequence of choosing independence from France, Leopold Sédar Senghor declared: "The choice of the Senegalese people is independence; they want it to take place only in friendship with France, not in dispute."

From then on France accepted only an "independence on paper" for its colonies, but they signed binding "Cooperation Accords" detailing the nature of their relations with France. Below are the 11 main components of the Colonization Continuation Pact since the 1950s:

#1. Colonial Debt for the benefits of France's colonization.

The newly "independent" countries should pay for the infrastructure built by France in the country during colonization. [If this seems blatantly bald-faced, know that] France made Haiti pay the modern equivalent of $21 billion from 1804 till 1947(!) for the losses caused to French slave traders by the abolition of slavery and the liberation of the Haitian slaves.

#2. Automatic confiscation of national reserves.

The African countries should deposit their national monetary reserves into France's Central Bank.

France has been holding the national reserves of fourteen African countries since 1961: Benin, Burkina Faso, Guinea-Bissau, Ivory Coast, Mali, Niger, Senegal, Togo,

Cameroon, Central African Republic, Chad, Congo-Brazzaville, Equatorial Guinea and Gabon.

Under the terms of the agreement . . . the Central Bank of each African country is obliged to keep at least 65% of its foreign exchange reserves in an "*operations account*" held at the French Treasury, as well as another 20% to cover financial liabilities.

The countries themselves do not know, nor are they told, how much of the pool of foreign reserves held by the French Treasury belongs to them as a group or individually [nor how the money is invested nor what it's earned or lost; and their access to the money is severely restricted].

It's now estimated that France is holding close to $500 billion of African countries' money in its treasury.

Former President Chirac recently spoke about the African nations' money in French banks: "We have to be honest, and acknowledge that a big part of the money in our banks comes precisely from the exploitation of the African continent."

#3. Right of first refusal on any raw or natural resource discovered in the country.

France has the first right to buy any natural resources found in the land of its ex-colonies.

#4. Priority to French interests and companies in public procurement and public bidding.

In the award of government contracts, French companies must be considered first. It doesn't matter if the African countries can obtain better value for their money elsewhere.

As a consequence, in many of the French ex-colonies, all the major economic assets of the countries are in the hands of the French. In Côte d'Ivoire, for example, French companies own and control all the major utilities – water, electricity, telephone, transport, ports and major banks. The same in commerce, construction, and agriculture.

#5. Exclusive right to supply military equipment and train the country's military officers.

Through a sophisticated scheme of scholarships, grants, and "Defense Agreements" attached to the Colonial Pact, the Africans should send their senior military officers for training in France or French-run training facilities.

The situation on the continent now is that France has trained hundreds, even thousands, of traitors and nourishes them. They are dormant when they are not needed, and activated when needed for a coup or any other purpose!

#6. Right for France to pre-deploy troops and intervene militarily in the country to defend its interests.

Under something called "Defence Agreements" attached to the Colonial Pact, France has the legal right to intervene militarily in the African countries, and also to station troops permanently in bases and military facilities in those countries, run entirely by the French.

#7. Obligation to make French the official language of the country and the language for education.

#8. Obligation to use French colonial money, the FCFA.

#9. Obligation to send France annual balance and reserve report.

No report, no money.

#10. Renunciation of the right to enter into military alliance with any other country unless authorized by France.

#11. Obligation to ally with France in a situation of war or global crisis.

France's unconscionable and savage repression of the 1950s-60s independence movements ensured, deliberately, Africa's *current* abject dependence, continuing almost seamlessly the flow of wealth out of Africa by adjusting the methods of extraction and forms of control (but always still with the military backing it up). For this current exploitation we have not heard any apology from French president Macron, who must be familiar with all the above details, and more. Apparently, he isn't interested in acknowledging that France, along with the rest of the handful of imperialist countries, HAS NEVER stopped its pillage of Africa, except to the extent that it's sucked all it can get from some areas. (And all while forever pretending to be trying to help it; that hasn't changed.) And why should we expect otherwise? Capitalism, whether in the form of slavery, colonialism, or, for the last 60 years, "neo"-colonialism, *has always* hunted down and captured cheap labor and demanded unrestricted access to raw materials and markets, all while "spiritually" buoyed by the self-serving mantra that the ends (so-called "growth and progress") justify the means, which include invasion, bombs, and torture. It's difficult for those of us who aren't global finance capitalists to fathom such a callously criminal approach to the world's people and its natural resources. But it has proven to be the nature of the beast.

Examples of the workings of this indirect, "neo"-colonialism abound. This from a 2006 presentation by Tanzanian politician, Humphrey Polepole:

Nowhere in Africa were positive contributions made to any substantial extent by colonialism. Countries like Nigeria and Ghana, which were among the better-endowed colonies, were left with only a few rail lines, rudimentary infrastructure and a few thousand graduates. This was better than in other places. The Portuguese, for instance, left their colonies with very little. At independence in 1975, Mozambique had only three dozen graduates.

Since the countries were just establishing themselves, the need for finances to improve the physical and social infrastructures was inevitable and that was the hook that trapped most political figures of those times in the post-colonial era. When we talk of economic development in the underdeveloped countries, we cannot avoid talking about the growing burden of debts as they pay billions of dollars every year while diverting the resources from the priority sectors such as health and education. UNICEF's 2000 report says that 30,000 children die *each day* due to poverty. That is just under 11 million children each year.

International instruments of trade and finance oversee a complex system of multilateral trade laws and financial agreements that keep the poor in their Bantustans. Its whole purpose is to institutionalize inequity. . . . A Christian Aid newsletter weighs in on this with a more recent report noting that sub-Saharan Africa is a massive $272 billion worse off because of "free" trade policies forced on them as a precondition for receiving aid and debt relief. They also note that the economic reforms that rich countries forced on Africa were supposed to boost economic growth. However, the reality is that imports increased massively while exports went up only slightly, which, further, didn't compensate African producers for the loss of local markets and, thus, they were left worse off.

It is such a pity when you realize . . . human beings are dying of hunger, malnutrition, and absolute poverty in the underdeveloped countries, obtaining under a dollar per day!!! Where is the human dignity?

And this from a 2011 article written for the *Washington Post* by Alex Dupuy, Haitian professor and author, a year after the devastating earthquake hit Haiti:

The laudable immediate humanitarian response [by the people of the world] to post-earthquake Haiti is one thing.

The objectives of the international community---the United States, Canada, and France; the United Nations; and financial institutions such as the World Bank and the International Monetary Fund---are quite another, and they're significantly more problematic. Their objectives and their policies first and foremost aim to benefit their own investors, farmers, manufacturers and nongovernmental organizations (NGOs).

The 1,000 or so foreign NGOs that are operating in Haiti . . . work independently of the Haitian government, reinforcing the country's dependence on foreign aid, and further sapping the capacity . . . of the government to meet the basic needs of its citizens.

The stage for this increased dependence . . . was set in the 1970s, when the international community, in particular the United States and the World Bank, devised development strategies that turned Haiti into the supplier of the region's cheapest labor for the garment industry. Haiti also went from producing 80 percent of its food in the 1980s to being one of the largest importers of U.S. food in the hemisphere today. This shift took place through "structural adjustment" policies that kept wages low and removed tariffs and some restrictions on imports. This was highly profitable for the foreign investors and their Haitian contractors, but the garment industry did little to reduce unemployment or lift its workers out of poverty.

One primary architect of the policy knows it wasn't a success. In testimony last March, former U.S. president, Bill

Clinton, co-chair of the U.S.-conceived Interim Haiti Recovery Commission, said that compelling Haiti to cut tariffs on imported rice from the United States "may have been good for some of my farmers in Arkansas, but it has not worked to help Haiti. It was a mistake." Later he acknowledged that the policies have "failed everywhere they've been tried." [The results of those policies---poverty, inequality, and social strife for underdeveloped countries, sterling financial rewards for foreign investors, lenders, and growers, not only for their immediate enrichment but to maintain the utter dependence of the former colonial countries---are exactly why those policies have been, and are, uniformly pushed across the 3rd World continents, Bill Clinton's personal candidness aside. After all, he was a major propagator of such policies during his two-term presidency of the 1990s.]

In July, 1944, as the Allied powers, mainly the U.S. and Britain, anticipated victory in WWII, a conference was held at the Bretton Woods resort deep in the woods of New Hampshire. There, the Bretton Woods Institutions (BWIs)---the World Bank and the International Monetary Fund---were formed. They announced the beginning of the U.S. dollar-dominated, global economic world order, and these two institutions were established to monitor it and tend to it in very financially concrete ways, mainly meaning, in practice, ensuring lending governments and banks of the safety of their investments in, and loans to, debtor nations. (Of course, in the case of poor and dependent debtor nations, this is presented as helping the debtor countries "develop.") The BWIs were also conceived as major economic tools in the looming Cold War, intending to keep war-ravaged countries in the capitalist orbit.

From a June, 2019 critique by *The Bretton Woods Project*:

Volumes of documents testify to the experiences of millions of people negatively impacted by their policies and programs. Together they suggest that the Bank and Fund's policies have failed to achieve their *stated* objectives [emphasis in original] and instead support an economic order that benefits elites and private sector interests at the expense of poor and marginalized communities.

Indeed, both the Bank and the IMF have faced and continue to face resistance and mobilizations from civil society and social movements, from the global 1994 "50 Years Is Enough" campaign, to the 2018 "People's Global Conference Against IMF-World Bank."

The on-going, blatant and shameless abuse of the 3rd World has been so embarrassing as to cause the mainstream media and even the World Trade Organization to at least jerk the chain of capitalism's big agriculture and its government. This from a May, 2004 editorial in the Cleveland *Plain Dealer*:

Acting on complaints filed by Brazil and most of the world's other cotton-producing nations, the World Trade Organization last week found that America's 125,000 or so cotton producers received nearly $4 billion in subsidies, both direct and indirect [which shattered the maximum amount allowable by the rules of the WTO].

This is the first time the WTO has challenged a rich nation's agricultural subsidies, and it should give Big Agriculture and the Big Government that inflates it, both here and in hugely subsidized Europe as well, cause to worry. Those rich nations combine for about $300 billion in such subsidies. And that's one of the reasons why so many small nations both fear and hate us. Our tax-payer-provided largesse to a relative handful of commodities producers makes it impossible for farms in impoverished countries to exist, let alone compete.

If the United States and the other large agriculture underwriters would just reduce---or better yet, eliminate---those subsidies, the World Bank estimates that 144 million people around this planet could lift themselves from poverty. But so far, most of the 535 people in Congress and the man in the White House have considered their own continued government employment to be of far greater concern. The hunger of those frustrated millions isn't nearly as important as cultivating the campaign contributions and votes of the cushioned crop growers. The rules of international cooperation pale before the rule of the dollar.

A little over a year later, the *New York Times* chimed in. This from an August, 2005 editorial:

The very same representatives of the club of rich countries who go around the world hectoring the poor to open up their markets to free trade put up roadblocks when those countries ask the rich to dismantle their own barriers to free trade in agricultural products.

The developed world funnels nearly $1 billion a day in subsidies to its own farmers, encouraging overproduction, which drives down commodity prices. Poor nations' farmers cannot compete with subsidized products, even within their own countries. In recent years, American farmers have been able to dump cotton, wheat, rice, corn and other products on world markets at prices that do not begin to cover their cost of production, all thanks to politicians and at the expense of American taxpayers. Europe's system, meanwhile, is even more odious: United States farm subsidies are equal to only a third of the European Union's.

Tariffs are also a problem. Take cocoa, for instance. European tariffs on raw material are lower than tariffs on final products. That means that cocoa-producing countries like Ghana can't export chocolate to Europe and are forced instead to just export the raw material, cocoa.

At this point, the reader might recognize the above example of cocoa as glaring evidence that one of the basic tenets of the old, colonial relationship---thou shalt not manufacture nor refine---is still in effect but, rather than through the old, direct rule by fiat, it is imposed by the entangled method of unequal tariffs/subsidies, private foreign investment, poverty, loans/debt, contractual obligations, and the ever-ready threat of coup or invasion. The colonial relationship itself was never conceived to be temporary, and its enforced underdevelopment of Africa, Asia, and Latin America continues unabated. It has, for hundreds of years, proven to be a "natural" consequence for capitalism's limitless "growth and progress" in North America, Western Europe, and, also, Japan.

Joan E. Spero and Jeffrey A. Hart do a broad study of the workings of the post-WWII global economy in the 2010 edition of their book, *The Politics of International Economic Relations*, where, among other things, they summarize the arguments and the evidence presented by critics of the role of multinational corporations (MNCs) in 3rd World countries:

A new body of analysis of MNCs emerged [in the 1970s] . . . that argued that policies encouraging inflows of foreign direct investments [FDIs] were not necessarily good for the population of the host states and that the multinationals

exploited the developing countries and perpetuated their dependence on the North.

MNCs did not bring in as much foreign capital [absolutely crucial for buying essential imports and paying on their debts] as their proponents suggested. The financing of foreign investment was done largely with host-country, not foreign, capital. For example, between 1958 and 1968, U.S. manufacturing subsidiaries in Latin America obtained 80 percent of all their financing locally. Furthermore, MNCs, because of their strength, often have preferred access [lower borrowing rates] to local capital sources and are able to compete successfully with, and thus stifle, local entrepreneurs. Such local financing is often used by the MNCs to acquire existing nationally owned firms.

One study of the Mexican economy revealed that 43 percent of U.S. MNCs entered Mexico by acquiring existing firms and that 81 percent of these firms were formerly owned by Mexicans. And in Brazil, 33 percent of U.S. MNCs began operations in Brazil by acquiring local firms. In the late 1960s and early 1970s, acquisitions accounted for 50 percent of the new multinational affiliates in Brazil, 63 percent of which were formerly owned by Brazilians.

Foreign investment in developing countries actually led to a net outflow of capital. Capital flows from South to North occurred through repatriation of profits, debt service, payment of royalties and fees [on the use of technology], and illicit manipulation of import and export prices. . . . In the 1970s, profits in developing countries were substantially higher than profits in developed market economies. The average return on U.S. private investment in the developed market economies between 1975 and 1978 was 12.1 percent, whereas the average return in developing countries was 25.8 percent. . . . Rates of return in some developing countries, in 1980, reached 41.3%.

Trade was identified as yet another mechanism of capital outflow in which MNCs disguised profits and evaded taxes. Much of the trade by multinational subsidiaries in developing countries was intracompany trade. Often, subsidiaries located in developing countries were obliged by agreements with the parent to purchase supplies from and make sales to the parent. The parent thus was able to manipulate the price of such intracompany imports and exports to benefit the firm. The firms then used their position to underprice exports and overprice imports, thereby invisibly shifting profits from the South to the North. In one study . . . it was argued that the overpricing of pharmaceutical imports into Colombia amounted to $3 billion.

The negative effects of such decapitalization might have been limited if, in the process of removing capital, the MNCs had made a significant contribution to local development. Critics contended that the contribution of MNCs was limited or negative . . . including having only a small effect on employment.

In sum, multinational corporations created a distorted and undesirable form of growth. They often created highly developed enclaves that did not contribute to the expansion of the larger economy. . . . In welfare terms, the benefits of the enclave accrued to the home country and to a small part of the host population allied with the corporation. Not only did the enclave not contribute to local development, said the critics, but it often hindered it. It absorbed local capital, removed capital from the country, destroyed local entrepreneurs, and created inappropriate consumer demands that turned production away from economically and socially desirable patterns [like reclaiming self-sufficiency in food staples].

As if to give voice to the reality of the above summation, this from an April, 2000 article in the *Third World Network*, reporting on a speech by the Malaysian prime minister describing the experience of his and other countries in the 1998 Asian crisis, caused by the flagrant and massive manipulation of the flow of foreign capital:

We had welcomed globalization believing it could help our economies grow. But in East Asia, rogue currency traders devalued the currencies, throwing millions out of work. The international institutions [World Bank and International Monetary Fund] moved in ostensibly to help with loans but in reality to facilitate the takeover of the countries' economy and even politics. All this is made possible because the rich interpret globalization as the right of capital to cross and re-cross borders at will.

Capital is the new gunship of the rich. By coming in with short term investments they create an illusion of wealth. Once that has happened they merely have to pull out their capital in order to impoverish and weaken their victims and force them to submit to foreign dictates.

He added that if globalization implies economic integration of all countries, why should it mean only the free flow of capital but not workers? If money is capital for the rich, labor is the capital of poor countries. Their workers should be allowed to migrate to rich countries to compete for jobs there, just as the powerful corporations of the rich are allowed to compete with their tiny counterparts in poorer countries.

If it is right for big corporations of the rich to displace small weak corporations of the poor, why is it so wrong for poor workers to displace workers in the rich countries?

He said the economic turmoil in East Asia has resulted in the rich taking what belongs to the poor. As banks and businesses collapse and share prices plunge, the rich move in to buy the devalued shares and acquire the companies.

They could have bought at normal prices during normal times but they preferred to emasculate us before they take over at a fraction of the cost. Backing this move are the international institutions which insist we open up so that the predators can move in and take over everything. [They say 3rd World] governments must not protect local businesses. Market forces must prevail, and those with money will dominate.

The market forces have had no noticeable success [for us] but have made fortunes for rich countries by their manipulations and by acquiring banks, industries and businesses.

No one knows global capitalism like its victims know it. Countless confrontations and crises throughout the 3rd World testify to that.

An example from an April 20th, 2008 article written by Anuradha Mittal for *Progressive Media Project*:

Food riots are erupting all over the world. In the last 30 years, developing countries that used to be self-sufficient in food have turned into large food importers.

Over the last few decades, the United States, the World Bank and the International Monetary Fund have used their leverage to impose devastating policies on developing countries. By requiring countries to open up their agriculture markets to giant multinational companies and by persuading [or requiring] them to specialize in exportable cash crops such as coffee, cocoa, cotton, and even flowers, Washington, the IMF and the World Bank created a downward spiral.

They made matters worse by demanding the dismantling of marketing boards that kept commodities in a rolling stock to be released in event of a bad harvest. These boards shielded both producers and consumers against sharp rises or drops in prices. But the shield is no longer there. . . . We need to stop worshiping the golden calf of the so-called free market and embrace instead the principle of food sovereignty. Every country and every people have a right to food that is affordable.

Percentage of budgets spent on food by the poorest one-fifth of households in the   United States: 16 percent.

Percentage of budgets spent on food by households in Indonesia: 50 percent.

Percentage of budgets spent on food by households in Vietnam: 65 percent.

Percentage of budgets spent on food by households in Nigeria: 73 percent.

Percentage increase in the price of corn in the last two years: 200 percent.

Percentage increase in the price of rice in the last three years: 250 percent.

Dried mud cookies in Port-au-Prince, Haiti---made of dirt, salt, and vegetable shortening---are one of very few options the poorest people have to stave off hunger.

As a result, food riots erupted in Egypt, Guinea, Haiti, Indonesia, Mauritania, Mexico, Senegal, Uzbekistan, and Yemen. For the 3 billion people in the world who subsist on $2 a day or less, the leap in food prices is a killer.

These sharp price fluctuations in life's essential commodities are entirely a function of a global capitalist economic system (as are depressions, recessions, inflations, stagnations, stagflations, etc.), not some "natural" phenomena, and, given the misery they cause, are in themselves grounds for banning that system that spawns them.

And this from an April 21st, 2005 report in the Cleveland Plain Dealer:

Lawmakers in Ecuador voted to remove President Lucio Gutierrez, a close U.S. ally, from office after a week of escalating street protests demanding his ouster. . . . Demonstrations surged over the past week and late one night 30,000 marched on the palace. . . . His [downfall came] after he instituted austerity measures, including cuts in food subsidies and cooking fuel, to satisfy international lenders.

From a June, 2018 Cleveland *PD* article:

Jordan's King Abdullah II accepted the resignation of his embattled prime minister and reportedly tapped a leading reformer as a successor, hoping to quell the largest anti-government protests in recent years, which are also seen as a potential challenge to the King's two-decade-old rule. . . . Prime Minister Hani Mulki's resignation came after several days of mass protests across Jordan against a planned tax increase, the latest in a series of economic reforms sought by the International Monetary Fund to get the rising public debt "under control" [my quotation marks]. The government has also raised prices for bread, electricity and fuel.

From an *Associated Press* article of July, 2004:

The fate of Bolivia's immense natural gas reserves was at stake in a referendum. . . . The issue is a sensitive one in Bolivia. Nine months ago, then-President Sanchez de Lozada was ousted for planning to export liquefied natural gas. Clashes between highland Indians and security forces in and around La Paz [the capital] left nearly 60 dead.

Lured by privatization of the industry, some 20 foreign companies have invested $3.5 billion in exploration, discovering 55 trillion cubic feet of gas. But some Bolivians remained wary of the [referendum] vote, as well as pledges that the exploitation of natural gas will raise incomes in a nation where two-thirds of the population live in poverty.

The gas reserves have split the nation, with Indians in the western Andean plains pitted against the business elite in the eastern and southern lowlands, where the gas reserves are located. The business leaders are set on exportation and have threatened to break away from the republic. Indian leaders in the west want the entire gas industry nationalized to ensure that profits stay in the country, an option that new president Carlos Mesa left off the ballot.

Less than a year later in Bolivia, a June 8th, 2005 *Associated Press* article reported:

Violent street protests choked off Bolivia's crippled capital as President Carlos Mesa's government collapsed. . . . Riot police fired tear gas, and miners, who joined protesting Indians, farmers, and laborers, responded by setting off sticks of dynamite. Army troops took up defensive positions around the Government Palace, the scene of clashes that capped weeks of opposition to Mesa's U.S.-backed, free-market government.

Washington has watched with concern for its free-market agenda, which has failed to ease the grinding poverty that affects 64 percent of Bolivians. The poverty has fueled anger at the U.S.-driven globalization movement.

And this from an October 31st, 2019 Cleveland *Plain Dealer* article:

Chilean President Sebastian Pinera said that he is canceling two major international summits so he can respond to protracted nationwide protests over economic inequality that have left more than a dozen people dead, hundreds injured and businesses and infrastructure damaged. The decision to call off the [summits] dealt a major blow to

Chile's image as a regional oasis of stability and economic development. Pinera said he was forced to cancel both events due to the chaos unleashed by 12 days of protests.

And from an August 7th, 2003 *Associated Press* article:

Rock-throwing protesters clashed with riot police in front of Brazil's Congress building. The march by an estimated 50,000 government workers started peacefully, but it ended in violence after hundreds broke through police barricades. . . . The protest was the largest gathering in the Brazilian capital since the Jan. 1 inauguration of President Lula da Silva, the country's first elected leftist leader.

The demonstration came hours after Brazil's Congress approved a key constitutional reform that would slash civil servants' pensions and save the government billions of dollars . . . frustrating people who voted for Silva---a former union leader. Silva has received widespread praise from investors for putting in place conservative economic policies but is under fire from radical elements of his Workers Party. . . . Protesters carried signs saying "Traitor, Get Out Mister Lula" and "The Government Is Kneeling Before Capitalism."

The opposition to capitalism, either in name or in substance, by the masses in 3rd World continents is entrenched in the electoral politics of those heavily-indebted countries. It's been commonplace for politicians to campaign on a position of such opposition only to accede to "an offer they can't refuse" when in office. Two short examples:

From an April, 1992 article in the Cleveland *Plain Dealer*:

Alberto Fujimori ran successfully for the Peruvian presidency on a vague program of "Work, Technology, and Honor." He attacked opponent Vargas Llosa's announced plans for harsh austerity measures. But within days of taking office, he implemented belt-tightening measures more drastic even than those envisioned by his opponent.

And from a January, 2006 *Associated Press* article:

Backing away from his tough campaign talk against U.S.-sponsored trade initiatives, Bolivian President-elect Evo Morales said he no longer rules out a free-trade deal with the United States. The leftist cocoa grower . . . said in an interview with The Associated Press that he is now open to the idea of joining a pact he strongly opposed as recently as November. "I understand that governing is doing good business for your people," he said. The comments seemed to be further evidence that Morales is softening his stance against the free market policies he railed against during his campaign.

As a New York Times March, 2005 article, reporting on the trend of "leftist" leaders in Latin America, quoted the director of the Latin American and

Caribbean Center, "You have to see much of what is said as good use of communications for the purpose of maintaining their popularity. It's a domestic rhetorical game, but when they are put against the wall, they have to make pragmatic decisions."

In fact, many Third World countries have the word "socialism" in their formal names, and/or in the name of the political party currently elected to power, and/or the word is mentioned in their Constitutions as the goal of their societies. But more than representing any substance of socialism, it is testimony to, and the shattered remnants of, their long and unsuccessful attempts to escape the clutches of global capitalism, and symbolic of the hopes they still have.

There is a widely-held belief that food and other essential commodities in the 3rd World are *so* cheap that a couple of dollars a day is all that's necessary on which to raise a family. Evidence to the contrary is readily available. This from a March 17th, 2018 article in *The Economist* magazine:

The World Bank publishes rough estimates of price levels in different countries, showing how far a dollar would stretch if converted into local currency. On this measure, Kenya is more expensive than Poland. . . . The relative cost of food,

compared with other goods, is higher in poor countries. In Africa, the absolute cost is sometimes high, too. Nigerians would save 30% of their income if they bought their food at Indian prices. Meat costs more in Ghana than in America.

And this, from a *New York Times* September 2nd, 2008 editorial:

There is a lot more poverty in the world than previously thought. The World Bank reported in August that in 2005, there were 1.4 billion people living below the [extreme] poverty line, that is, living on less than $1.25 a day. That is more than a quarter of the developing world's population and 430 million more people living in extreme poverty than previously estimated. ... The poverty estimate soared after a careful study of the prices people in developing countries pay for goods and services revealed that the World Bank had been grossly underestimating the cost of living in the poorest nations for decades. As a result, it was grossly overestimating the ability of people to buy things. And the new research doesn't account for the soaring prices of energy and food in the past two years. The poverty expressed in the World Bank's measure is so abject that it is hard for citizens of the industrial world to comprehend.

But, are things actually getting better for 3rd World countries? In August, 2008, the *NY Times* carried a Reuters article reporting that, according to the World

Bank, in 1981 there were 1.9 billion people on the Asian, African, and Latin American continents, 52% of their total population, enduring the *extreme* poverty (the Bank's poorest category) of income under $1.25 per day. However, that 1.9 billion figure for 1981 is higher than the 1.4 billion 25 years later in 2005 (cited in the *NYT* article just above). That reported statistical reduction in the number of people in extreme poverty has been the fodder for some major U.S. mainstream media journalists to deliriously sing hallelujahs to global capitalism (to which we will return).

The World Bank has four poverty levels for the 3rd World. The most recent ones were set in 2015. The lowest level, "extreme" or "absolute" poverty, which means living on the edge of starvation, is now set at less than $1.90 per day (up from $1.25 per day). The other three levels, still in poverty, range from $10 per day down to $1.90. Using this wider designation of poverty rather than only the "extreme" worst, the World Bank's chart shows that from 1981 to 2005 there was virtually no change in the world distribution of wealth and poverty: 25% rich, 75% poverty stricken. The available world poverty statistics swirl and can sometimes confound, but only the blind and/or biased can put an overall positive spin on them, as well as on the prospects for the future of the people of the 3rd World under global capitalism. After all, that system is what put them in such generations-long dire circumstances in the first place.

But, for our swooning journalists:

Never mind that the WB reports that, "Forty-two percent of the people of India live below the poverty line . . . and it has more people in extreme poverty than it did 25 years ago." Never mind that, according to the above August, 2008 Reuters article, "Half of the people in sub-Saharan Africa were living below the poverty line in 2005, the same as in 1981. Never mind that, according to the March, 2005 *NY Times* article cited above, referring to Latin America, "Over the past decade, freer trade and increased foreign investment have failed to narrow the gap between rich and poor and left millions of poor people outside the economy and looking in resentfully. Between 1998 and 2003, once inflation is taken into account, Latin America as a whole did not grow at all, according to International Monetary Fund figures."

In fact, the World Bank data say that now there are 1.39 billion *more* people in poverty in the 3rd World than there were in 1981. And, further in fact, the U.N.-affiliated International Labor Organization, in a press release of June, 2000, stated: "The number of people living in *extreme* poverty around the world has *increased* by 200 million people in just the last five years, mainly in sub-Saharan Africa, Central Asia, Eastern Europe and Southeast Asia."[Our italics] And never mind that, because of the "monoculture" of dependence on very few raw materials or crops for export that global capitalism has forced upon them, extreme market price fluctuations for those commodities have repeatedly wiped out any "prosperity" they might have temporarily achieved, not only throwing them deeper into poverty, but into mass starvation. As the World Bank writes on one of its websites, "Moreover, for those who have been able to move out of poverty, progress is often temporary: Economic shocks, food insecurity and climate change threaten to rob them of their hard-won gains and force them back into poverty."

And never mind that the WB also tells us, "Access to good schools, health care, electricity, safe water, and other critical services remains elusive for many people. . . . The multidimensional view—wherein [such] aspects are included—reveals a world in which poverty is a much broader, more entrenched problem. The share of poor according to this multidimensional definition is approximately 50 percent higher than when relying solely on monetary poverty."

So, you'll excuse them if the people of the 3rd World don't form a transcontinental conga line to celebrate the announcement by our journalists of their being "lifted out of poverty."

None of the above information dampens our journalists' ecstatic odes to, and distortions of, capitalism. Their target is the minds of the people of the U.S., especially the youth, whom they are tasked with keeping from drifting intellectually away from capitalism and toward socialism (as part of the movement of support for self-described Democratic Socialist Bernie Sanders' presidential campaigns, in both 2016 and 2020; Sanders' campaigns, even while Sanders himself stated his support for capitalism, made the major media feel unique pressure to defend the honor of their system).

One can almost hear their clinking glasses as they celebrate the World Bank statistics, and treat us to the classic, ivory-towered, idealist view of capitalism. These few lines from one of them, an April, 2016 article by *Washington Post* editorial columnist Charles Lane entitled, "A 'moral economy' sounds nice, but capitalism helps real people," help make the point:

Lane trumpets "this historic progress, with its overwhelmingly beneficial consequences for millions of the world's humblest inhabitants."
  And:

"This was a process mightily abetted by freer flows of international trade and private capital. . . ."

And:

"The extension of capitalism fueled economic growth . . . ."

If Lane wanted us to see things from the point of view of the people of the 3rd World, he would have written, "The extension of capitalism, abetted by freer flows of international trade and private capital, was the curse of the southern hemisphere." In the historic and big picture, "the extension of capitalism fueled economic growth"... *for whom?*

And this from Lane's same column:

Capitalism comprises "the very engines of global growth and prosperity that helped lift hundreds of millions from a grinding and miserable poverty. . . ."

Again, to translate this from the language of the beneficiaries of capitalism into that of its victims, it would read, capitalism comprises "the very engines of global growth and prosperity that lifted hundreds of millions in Europe and North America to unimaginable wealth and comfort while, at the same time, imposing grinding and miserable poverty (and oppressive regimes) on the southern hemisphere."

And one wonders why Lane didn't bother to ask how it came to be in the first place that "hundreds of millions" were in a state of "grinding and miserable poverty" in 1981. Maybe it's because capitalism's "engines of global growth and prosperity" were very much in operation then (and long before then).

Lane allows, in passing, that some world events have "badly damaged capitalism's legitimacy," but he nonetheless insists we must "preserve [read: impose] 'free-market' institutions . . . while . . . curbing their excesses." Lane gives two examples of the "excesses" to which he refers: One, "the fact that the global '1 percent' . . . got a 60 percent boost in their real income over the past quarter-century certainly doesn't help matters, politically." And two, "the spectacular 2008 financial crisis that led to the Great Recession also badly damaged capitalism's legitimacy."

It is, indeed, capitalism's "legitimacy" (or, more accurately, *appearance* of legitimacy) with which Lane is deeply concerned, without a whiff of empathy for, or even acknowledgement of, the "excesses" of industrial exploitation of the hundreds of millions for whom he is so happy. The appalling conditions of life of those he uses as data with which he hopes to buttress people's faith in capitalism is not an "excess" with which Lane is concerned or, apparently, of which he is even aware.

And one more from Lane:

"Like any complex economic process, globalization was not all upside for everyone. . . ."

We include this one because it still stands as the grand-daddy of all understatements so far this century.

And we also have a contribution from David Brooks, *NYT* Opinion Columnist, in his article of December 5, 2019 on the same topic and for the same purpose, using the same World Bank statistics. Brooks first makes his toast: "Two cheers for capitalism, now and forever," and then informs us that:

"I came to realize that capitalism is really good at doing the one thing socialism is really bad at: creating a learning process to help people figure stuff out."

Never mind that history clearly shows that capitalism vigorously and consistently kept technological know-how out of reach of the people of the 3rd World, notoriously preventing them from manufacturing and withholding every patent from them and over them, deliberately consigning them to a lifetime of non-development and dependence. Again, the question is: "a learning process" to help *which* people figure stuff out?

And, in breathtaking obliviousness, Brooks gives us this gem:

"[The government] creates enormous misery when it cripples the motivational system that drives capitalism."

If Brooks meant for us to see things from the point of view of the hundreds of millions mired in poverty throughout the 3rd World, he'd easily have recognized and written that "the motivational system that drives capitalism" is competitively predatory and "creates enormous misery" for those it marks as its prey: cheap labor, and then cheaper labor still, about as close to slavery as they can get it. But, from the perspective of Brooks and his peers, capitalism's "motivational system" has delivered wonderful results.

And, also from Brooks' article, our personal favorite for winner of the Ivory-Tower Fantasy Award:

"Every year, hundreds of millions of people march with their feet to capitalism."

Someone should inform Mr. Brooks that those millions across Africa, Asia, and Latin America, marching hundreds of miles on foot, clawing at the borders of Europe and the U.S., risking and losing their lives in a desperate attempt to follow the wealth that's been sucked out of their countries and find a job, is *not* a joyous parade celebrating capitalism. Sorry to break that to him.

Brooks' article is entitled, "I Was Once a Socialist. Then I Saw How It Worked."

If Brooks understands how socialism works as well as he understands how capitalism works, we'll skip any lectures on the subject he might have planned.

Also, if Lane and Brooks feel the need to lobby for credit to be given capitalism for any statistical improvement, however slight, of the world's most impoverished and oppressed, they needn't bother. It is readily apparent that it could only have been a result of the "complex economic process of globalization" (Lane's formulation).

After all, global capitalism runs the world economy and has for a long, long time. So, let's take a look at an example of the main way capitalism produces any such present-day statistical improvements. This from the comprehensive article "Global Extreme Poverty" in *Our World in Data*, a non-partisan global research organization (using World Bank statistics), published in 2013, updated in 2017 and 2019:

Growing international trade has changed our world drastically. . . . One of its particular effects has been a substantial increase in the demand for industrial manufacturing workers in low income countries, mainly due to the rise in offshoring of low-skilled jobs. A common argument put forward is that these industrial manufacturing jobs are a powerful instrument for reducing poverty [and the first step on the path to development] even if salaries tend to be very low by the standards of rich countries.

A more careful analysis of the argument reveals a complex reality. On the one hand, low skilled industrial jobs do provide a formal, steady source of income, so it is possible that they raise incomes and reduce poverty. Yet, on the other hand, these jobs tend to be unpleasant and very poorly paid opportunities even by the standards of low income countries.

[After researchers did a study of foreign-owned or contracted factories and newly-hired workers in Ethiopia in 2016], "they found that these low-skill industrial jobs paid more than the alternatives available to a substantial fraction of workers; but at the same time, they had adverse health effects and did not offer a long-term solution—most applicants quit the formal sector quickly, finding industrial jobs unpleasant and risky."

So what did they find? Basically, that these are *bad jobs* [emphasis in original]. They hurt people's health and don't actually pay more than [some] other opportunities. "Yeah, it's better to have more jobs around — but there are actually some considerable health risks here. People are taking them because they're desperate."

Working in an industrial job [in the 3rd World] is associated with at least a 28 percentage point increase in perceived health risks (especially chemicals but also smoke), a more than 40 percentage point increase in the perception of a need for safety equipment, and at least a 35 percentage point increase in complaints of chemicals. [Recall the Bangladeshi, Indonesian, and Chinese factories, and their dismal pay and conditions, described earlier.]

The "sweatshops" label clearly hits on something true: These factories are more dangerous than other places to work, and don't pay enough to make up for those risks.

Let's meet some of the grateful "beneficiaries" about whom Lane and Brooks are paternally beaming. This from a February, 2015 report on a journey by three Norwegians touring the apparel industry in Asia. Their trip was arranged and taped by Norway's largest newspaper, *Aftenposten*:

Cambodian sweatshops have stunned Anniken Jorgenson. Anniken Jorgenson and three other individuals experienced a culture shock as they journeyed here to learn about apparel fashion. They learned of the dehumanizing work that people do in order to make a living for three dollars a day. The scholars are introduced to working in an environment that is mentally and physically exhausting and brought young Anniken to tears. The world they experienced is basically the Capitalist vampire. They are stuck in a place where it destroys you but keeps you alive, barely. The article explains that, with the three dollars they made after standing (because the chairs were uncomfortable), they managed to get soup and a couple of little pieces of chicken. This is what keeps them alive: you get a little light in a dark room but it destroys any thought process of striving to get more out of life other than bare necessities.

The only thing our journalists Lane and Brooks heard here is...they're making $3/day! That's way more than $1.90! What's not to like?! You can almost hear their glasses clinking again.

And, would Mr. Brooks, since he crows over the "historic progress" of exactly such people as those described above, like to offer the above as an example of what he praises as "the motivational system that drives capitalism"? Or did he have another, happier, version, one that only he knows about, in mind?

It's easy to see why Lane and Brooks will *not* be directing their glowing praise of the global "free" market to, say, the people of Guatemala. This from a January 6th, 2013 article in the *New York Times*:

On a recent morning, Jose Antonio Alvarado was harvesting his corn crop on the narrow median of Highway 2 as trucks zoomed by. "We're farming here because there is no other land, and I have to feed my family," said Mr. Alvarado.

Recent laws in the United States and Europe that mandate the increasing use of biofuel in cars have had far-flung ripple effects, economists say, as land once devoted to growing food for humans is now sometimes more profitably used for churning out vehicle fuel. In a globalized world, the expansion of the biofuels industry has contributed to spikes in food prices and a shortage of land for food-based agriculture in poor corners of Asia, Africa and Latin America because the raw material for biofuels is grown wherever it is cheapest. . . . With its corn-based diet and proximity to the United States, Central America has long been vulnerable to economic riptides related to the United States' corn policy. Now that the United States is using 40 percent of its crop to make biofuel, it is not surprising that tortilla prices have doubled in Guatemala, which imports nearly half of its corn.

At the same time, Guatemala's lush land, owned by a handful of families, has proven ideal for producing raw materials for biofuels. Suchitepequez Province, a major corn-producing region five years ago, is now carpeted with sugar cane and African palm. The field Mr. Alvarado used to rent for his personal corn crop now grows sugar cane for a company that exports bioethanol to Europe. In a country where most families must spend about two thirds of their income on food, "the average Guatemalan is now hungrier because of biofuel development," said a researcher for a Guatemalan nonprofit that studies rural issues. Roughly 50 percent of the nation's children are chronically malnourished, according to the United Nations.

"There are pros and cons to biofuel, but not here," said a labor union representative for Guatemala's farmers. "These people don't have enough to eat. They need food. They need land. They can't eat biofuel, and they don't drive cars."

The current American mandate, established in 2007 by Congress, can be waived by the Environmental Protection Agency but, according to law, such adjustments must focus on [U.S.] domestic issues like cases in which biofuel "requirements would severely harm the economy of a state, a region, or the United States," the agency said in an email when asked for comment. [In other words, there's no amount of harm the U.S. can do *to Guatemala* that could compel the U.S. to adjust its biofuel "requirements"!]

Once nearly self-sufficient in corn production, Guatemala became more dependent on imports in the 1990s as a surplus of subsidized American corn flowed south. Guatemalan farmers could not compete, and [local] corn production [plummeted]. But cheap imports disappeared once the United States started using corn to fulfill its 2007 biofuels standards. "The use of maize to make biofuel has led to these crazy prices," said the head of the United Nations World Food Program in Guatemala. It "is not ethically acceptable," he added. It is agency policy to buy corn locally, but there is no extra corn grown here anymore. And Guatemalans cannot go back to the land because so much of it is being devoted to growing crops for biofuel. (Almost no biofuel is used domestically.)

For Guatemala's largest landowners, long-term leases with large biofuel companies are more profitable and easier to manage than cattle ranching or renting to subsistence farmers. In small towns, a palm company is pressing farmers to lease their fields. "I'm trying not to because I need that land to grow corn," said one farmer. But he added that farming has become difficult as nearby plantations divert and deplete rivers to feed industrial-scale irrigation systems. Ash from burning cane fields after harvest also damages his corn crop and irritates his children's lungs, he said. In the remote Mayan villages in the north of the country, the incursion of plantations has brought a few good jobs and some training, but many complain of low wages and the back-breaking nature of the work. . . . With sometimes violent confrontations over land and labor, plantation gates are secured with armed guards.

Nor would our good journalists be directing their versions of capitalism to the people of Nigeria. From a February 24th, 2013 *NYT* article:

In Nigeria, at least 70 percent of the people live below the poverty line, and 80 percent of the country's oil wealth goes to 1 percent of the population. . . . "We can't rely on the government for water, light, security. Whatever you want, you have to provide for yourself," said a parish priest. For his parishioners, he said, "what they face is huge. So they tend to come to God as their last resort. You can't go to the police. Who will you go to? You will go to God. Some of them, where they sleep is so bad, they just come to sleep here during the day." After a devastating bus accident recently, the church paid parishioners' hospital bills, the priest said. "Otherwise they would die."

"The church offers the best schools, social services, and medicine. The God talk in Africa is a mark of the failure of the economic, social and political system," added a local bishop. "We are being called left, right, and center to mend the broken pieces of what are considered the failing states of Africa."

It should be noted that, from the perspective of U.S. and European banks and corporations, the economic system of which the bishop speaks was, and is, anything but a failure. It has perpetrated a massive extraction of wealth from Nigerian subsoil and labor, which was its intended purpose, marking it as a great success. The proof is in the overflowing coffers of multinational corporate industries and their governments' treasuries. (Certainly, our good journalists could find some "trickle down" effect for the people of Nigeria and raise a toast to it.)

From an April 28th, 2018 article in *The Economist* magazine:

Since 2000, the number of children who die before they are five has fallen by almost half. Life expectancy has reached 71. More children than ever are vaccinated. Malaria, TB, and HIV/AIDS are in retreat. Yet the gap between this progress and the still greater potential that medicine offers has perhaps never been wider.

At least half the world is without access to what the World Health Organization deems essential, including antenatal care, insecticide-treated bed nets, screening for cervical cancer and vaccinations against diphtheria, tetanus, and whooping cough. Safe, basic surgery is out of reach for 5 billion people [!] Those who can get to see a doctor often pay a crippling price.

It should be remembered that, as with the Nigerian church described above, any improved health care for people in the 3rd World does not happen because of the global capitalist system, if it happens at all. Quite the contrary, capitalism, over time, *causes* and leaves behind poor and sick people with little health structure. It is by the good graces of organizations like UNICEF (the U.N. children's fund), Doctors Without

Borders, Red Cross, etc. which fill in the social craters, such as the all-important vaccination of the children. Even if some corporate foundations contribute to the cost, that doesn't compensate for the fact that, when it comes to the 3rd World, the process of capitalism caused and enhanced the aching social deprivation, creating widespread and lasting social wounds, which are then left for humanitarian forces to try to solve, or at least somewhat alleviate.

And also from *The Economist*:

Almost one million people, 2/3 of them in Africa, still lack access to electricity, mainly because they can't afford to pay for it, according to the International Energy Agency, a research group. *The Economist*, in a December, 2017 issue, advises that, "Without industrialization and good jobs, few Africans will be able to afford much electricity."

Well, that pretty much seals it because industrialization and good jobs, under the very same economic world order that vigilantly prevented exactly that for hundreds of years, is a dream. Thus, for the same reason, Africans can only dream of universal access to electricity for as long as that system continues to run the world. There is no significant evidence to the contrary.

Ronald Steel, writing in 1967, could have been writing today when he summarized the economic and political relations that systematically dominate the world. From his book, *Pax Americana*:

The problems caused by political feudalism, social repression, and economic stagnation are so deep and their effects so widespread that chances for orderly and peaceful change in Latin America are not very bright. It is not simply that conditions are intolerable for the vast majority of Latin Americans, but that they are getting even worse. Today [1967] food consumption per inhabitant is less than it was twenty-five years ago. A good part of the continent is living on the edge of starvation. . . . [T]o the landless peasant and the slum-dwelling urban proletarian, political democracy as practiced in much of Latin America has not meant more than the freedom to be hungry and ill. . . .

Although formally independent, many of the underdeveloped countries are so tied into the Western economy (to the former mother countries of Europe, in the case of Africa; to the United States, in the case of Latin America) that an independent economic policy is virtually impossible. . . . It is this difference between the promise of political independence and the reality of Western economic control that the elites [the social, economic, and political leaders] of the new nations call "neo-colonialism" (208, 212, 263).

After having crushed their progress as self-sufficient, egalitarian civilizations, some of them far in advance of impoverished European societies at the time, hundreds of gruesome years later Western Europe and North America have disabled and famished three continents. Their time-tested neo-colonial formula goes like this: They are poor because they are paid so low, and they are paid so low because they are poor. Perfect! But this requires maintaining a vast army of unemployed and destitute labor, which keeps wages abysmal. Capitalism had already achieved this by enforced industrial non-development and monopolization of their land and their local markets over many years. And that sets up the other factor of the equation: Now that you all are harnessed, in your millions, to work as cheap labor for us, you will need to eat in order to keep working those long hours. And you will use your meager wages to buy that food, and other basic necessities, which are imported from us, thus completing the circle of exploitation.

And, to solder the yoke of dependency and keep the "arrangement" permanent, when your local rulers need a loan (which they will) in order to pay for that imported food (which they no longer can grow) and other necessities, we'll arrange for that, too, for the right collateral. And so it goes, on and on. To the lords of capital, this is the natural order of things. It's the order between parasite and host.

Much as they tout their "efforts" to do so, it's easy to see that international capitalism isn't in the business of "lifting the Third World out of poverty." They are in the business of *creating* that poverty, intentionally and unintentionally, for the purpose of their own enrichment. This is the big secret the top global financial firms, foundations, "think tanks," and corporations must guard with a show of "philanthropy," world conferences on "poverty reduction," and crocodile tears.

They can't even lift African-Americans out of poverty, not that their efforts at it are any more strenuous than they are for the people of the Third World. Poor Black, brown, white, and any other poor people in this country also act as an army of surplus labor, desperate for any wage to try to make ends meet and, as a predictable result, keeping low-wage industries in this country low-wage.

But this system has no present or future to offer millions of American Blacks, especially the youth, except poverty, unemployment, and prison. According to the Bureau of Justice Statistics, one in three Black men can expect to go to prison in their lifetime. Following their release, they might never find employment---and will often return to prison.

In 1968, the National Advisory Commission on Civil Disorders, appointed by President Lyndon Johnson to "search for the roots of the rising militancy in our country," called on the country in its *Report* to make "massive and sustained" investments in jobs and education to reverse the "segregation and poverty [that] have created in the racial ghetto a destructive environment totally unknown to most white Americans." Fifty years later, the Commission's lone surviving member concluded that "in many ways, things have gotten no better—or have gotten worse."

As yet another on-going U.S. example, according to the Federal Reserve Board, in 2016 the median wealth (including equity in a house) of Black families ($17,600) was about one-tenth that of white families ($171,000). And this existed at the end of a two-term administration of the first Black U.S. president. Capitalism is little affected by such politics.

This inequality, in all its many brutal and humiliating forms, becomes "normal" and, thus, tolerable, even expected, in the minds of successive generations of white people. Blacks' enforced inferior position becomes the "innate inferiority" of Blacks, just as water, the thinking goes, finds its "natural" level. Fundamentally, broad-based racism against Blacks is, to a large degree, the *result* of prolonged, deep inequality. And, thus, one cannot get rid of racism while, at the same time, leaving this profound inequality in place. Which means the system of capitalism in this country, which seized upon this subordination of Africans in the first place in order to enrich itself, and has presided over the continued subordination of African-Americans up to this moment, must be held responsible for the racism with which it has burdened Black people and, indeed, poisoned all of society.

And where racism is concerned, we should give "credit" where credit is due. One of the main perpetrators was, and still is, Thomas Jefferson. A major slave holder (much as he "lamented" slavery's unfortunate, "temporary" necessity), Jefferson wrote in his 1783 "Notes on the State of Virginia" a tract that still stands as the handbook, first of all for the justification of slavery, but, as a consequence, for the justification of racism against Blacks for all time. While it's too odious to reprint here, it's worth remembering that, when today's white supremacists look to the Founding Fathers for encouragement and "credibility," they are richly rewarded. It's a "gift" from the colonial grave that keeps on "giving."

Global capitalism has so tightly and intricately wrapped its tentacles around the world that it's like a stick: if you push one end, the other end moves. It can be seen, as one example, in the almost instantaneous price fluctuations in reaction to a sudden greater or lesser production of a commodity in one or another part of the world, with sudden food riots and even starvation of the people in the poor countries. Their daily lives and fate are far more determined by the United States' political and economic policies and actions than they are by their own governments. Thus, they should have the right to vote in U.S. presidential elections. Think of the campaign oratory that would produce. As it is, much as they all must be aware of the super-profits drained from the 3rd World nations and the resulting dismal conditions in these nations, there isn't even a mention, much less a protest, about it from U.S. presidential candidates. Instead, they all compete to be the loudest voice, with the "progressive" voices the loudest of all, demanding that a bigger share of the loot go to their voting constituencies (usually defined as the American middle class). Which among them hasn't or wouldn't declare their allegiance to, and defense of, the current world order and, most of all, the U.S.' position as the top dog in that order? After all, maintaining that order is the very job description of the position for which they're running---CEO of the most powerful capitalist class in the world. If there is any doubt about that, recall the advice out-going president Barack Obama gave in-coming president Donald Trump in his farewell letter. Among other, lesser, points, Obama wrote:

"It's up to us, through action and example, to sustain the international order that's expanded steadily since the end of the Cold War, and upon which our own wealth and safety depend."

And Obama certainly did his part. As written in August, 2016 by an approving editorial writer on national security for *Bloomberg View*:

In 2009 [Obama's first year in office], Obama was awarded the Nobel Peace Prize for his "vision of a world free from nuclear arms." It's one of the delicious ironies of the Barack Obama presidency that a man who came into office with lofty talk on nuclear nonproliferation would oversee the biggest modernization of the U.S. arsenal since the Cold War. His administration kick-started a $1 trillion nuclear upgrade initiative that, among other things, will refurbish eight major weapons labs and prolong the lives of the Pentagon's most important tactical nuclear bomb and submarine-based warhead. . . . Experience tends to make pragmatists of us all (Cleveland Plain Dealer, 8-7-16).

"If you say you're a capitalist, then the next thing you must say is, 'I compete.'" ----Donald Regan, Treasury Secretary for Ronald Reagan (Nomi Prins, *All The Presidents' Bankers*, 319).

The above quote is a concise statement of the capitalist creed which is, actually, a command by the inescapably competitive nature of their system.

Applied on a global scale over time, it has led to a grotesquely lopsided economic world with *billions* barely able to survive, and a globe bristling with armaments of mass destruction. In 2017, the world spent $1.7 trillion dollars on weapons systems. And, at the same time, and not coincidentally, their mantra of competition has been effectively foisted upon the population as an "indispensable" mechanism for motivating people to work for industrial and technical progress. This is one of the greatest ruses of all time, the most self-serving, and probably the most destructive. And, further, it calls into question just what "progress" for humanity actually is.

This is not the "civilization" the world is capable of reaching. Real civilization, where we cooperatively use the earth's resources, our accumulated technology, and our collective minds and labor power in common for the common good, capitalism can never bring, even though we have the technology to do it. But capitalism hires scientists to develop technology as privately owned and protected "intellectual property" for the purpose of competitive edge and personal enrichment.

Speaking especially with regard to Third World nations, the attraction of socialism, as shown in places earlier, has mainly been as a defense against the penetration and control by foreign capital and its local, heavily armed enforcers. And, thus, global capitalism, driven competitively to greater and greater accumulation of profit through expansion of capital investment, wherever the highest returns can be had, sees socialism, anywhere in the world, as an unacceptable shrinking and restricting of its available fields of exploitation, as well as a dangerous inspiration to other poor and oppressed people, and seeks to block it, by any means necessary. And, they're right: without their hawkish vigilance, and the work of their fascistic 3rd World strongmen, their worst fears for their parasitic system *would* eventually be realized---and justly so. Let's not forget: it was capitalism, not socialism, that harnessed slavery and turned it into a burgeoning global marketplace. It was capitalism that imposed the yoke of colonialism on virtually the entire continents of Africa, Asia, and Latin America all the way up to the middle of the 20th century. And it's been the rapaciousness of capitalism, not socialism, that's been behind just about every war waged for the last two hundred years. (And a close look at the European entanglement of WWII, the "good war" that slaughtered 60 million people, would show it to be fundamentally in that same category, as the sequel to WW I.)

EVEN IF socialism was the "evil" that capitalism desperately tries to paint it, it *still* could only dream of equaling the savage crimes against humanity of which capitalism is guilty.

A wise person once observed that sometimes the truth is so dangerous that it has to be guarded by a wall of lies. This precisely describes the predicament—and partial solution—for the major capitalist countries in the face of the earth-shaking socialist victory by a politically awakened and determined working class in Russia in 1917, inspiring revolutionary movements around the world: how to prevent the U.S. and European industrial working class, and the poor, exploited and oppressed workers of the southern continents, from embracing this new workers' fatherland. One could say this was the actual beginning of the "Cold War," with lurid tales of bestial, Bolshevik "terror" spewed upon the world's population. ("Bolshevik" means "majority," referring to the portion of the industrial working class of Russia that were members and adherents of its faction in the broad revolutionary movement against the long and harsh rule of the czar, and against Russia's continued participation in the imperialist slaughter of WW I.)

The wall of lies materialized immediately and was found more or less adequate for keeping their own generally more comfortable and, thus, more credulous citizens loyal and, for the most part, that "pact" has endured to this day. But, for the workers throughout the Third World continents, the imperial capitalists would have to rely more on the brute force of local gendarmes, coups, invasions, and massacres in order to keep their colonial and post-colonial treasure troves of raw materials and cheap labor out of the socialist sphere of influence and, as we are always told, "safe for democracy." This, then, was the fundamental and essential part of the Cold War as waged by the Western alliance, which rapidly accelerated following WWII. Perhaps the intrigue, the rival alliances, the sanctions, the tariffs, the diplomacy, the arms build up, etc., might be considered "cold" war. But that wasn't the part of the war with which the people of Latin America, Africa, and south and southeast Asia were saddled. For them, it was always hot, and still is. And always will be as long as this system of big-power competition running roughshod over the world continues to exist.

As it turned out, Russia's top rulers dragged their nation into the ranks of big capitalist powers vying for part of the U.S.' world-wide empire after betraying and abandoning the challenging road of socialism, beginning long before the official collapse of the USSR in 1991. However, while we're therefore not, of course, promoting what the Soviet Union/Russia was turned into as any "model" for the world, it's nonetheless instructive to hear from large numbers of those who lived the experience both before and after the disintegration of the USSR.

This from the on-line magazine, *Aeon*:

For those wishing to paint 20th-century communism as an unmitigated evil, ongoing ethnographic and survey research in Eastern Europe contradicts any simple narrative. . . . As governments dismantled social safety nets and poverty spread throughout the region, ordinary citizens grew increasingly less critical of their state socialist pasts.

A 2009 poll in eight East European countries asked if the economic situation for ordinary people was "better, worse or about the same as it was under communism." The results stunned observers: 72 per cent of Hungarians and 62 per cent of both Ukrainians and Bulgarians believed that most people were *worse* off after 1989 [emphasis in original]. In no country did more than 47 per cent of those surveyed agree that their lives improved after the advent of free markets. Subsequent polls and qualitative research across Russia and Eastern Europe confirm the persistence of these sentiments as popular discontent with the failed promises of free-market prosperity has grown.

These poll results aren't so surprising when one considers the damage done, in the immediate wake of the collapse of the Soviet Union, from the swooping in like vultures by the instruments of world capitalism. Throughout Eastern Europe, Russia, and the ex-Soviet republics, the World Bank and International Monetary Fund (IMF), and the banks and governments behind them, imposed strict and austere SAPs (economic "structural adjustment programs"), the same ones they always plant in weakened and vulnerable countries, as the price for the approval of loans. And the people reap the same things—rising poverty, soaring inequality, loss of social security, massive debt, and an economy that fluctuates like the worldwide weather from week to week. But international capitalism, if it's "successful," reaps fortunes from the privatization of almost everything in the country, above ground and below ground, not to mention the mammoth revenue from the imposed burden of servicing the debt.

(Amid much documentation of this phenomenon by analysts, the IMF has posted a highly detailed report on its website of its painstaking efforts to establish these SAPs in Russia during the 1990s.)

And to top it all off---from the article, "Crude Awakening," *The Economist* magazine, February, 2019:

In America, the world's largest economy and its second biggest polluter, climate change is becoming hard to ignore. Extreme weather has grown more frequent. In November, wildfires scorched California; last week Chicago was colder than parts of Mars. Scientists are sounding the alarm more urgently and people have noticed---73% of Americans polled by Yale University late last year said that climate change is real. The left of the Democratic Party wants to put a "Green New Deal" at the heart of the election in 2020. As expectations shift, the private sector is showing signs of adapting. Last year around 20 coal mines shut. Fund managers are prodding firms to become greener. Warren Buffett . . . is staking $30 billion on clean energy and Elon Musk plans to fill America's highways with electric cars.

Yet amid the clamor is a single, jarring truth. Demand for oil is rising and the energy industry, in America and globally, is planning multi-trillion-dollar investments to satisfy it. No firm embodies this strategy better than ExxonMobil. It plans to pump 25% more oil and gas in 2025 than in 2017. If the rest of the industry pursues even modest such growth, the consequences for the climate could be disastrous.

In 2000 BP promised to go "beyond petroleum" and, on the face of it, the majors [ExxonMobil, BP, Chevron, Royal Dutch Shell, and Total] have indeed changed. All say that they support the Paris agreement to limit climate change and all are investing in renewables such as solar. Shell recently said that it would curb emissions from its products. Yet ultimately you should judge companies by what they do, not what they say.

According to ExxonMobil, global oil and gas demand will rise by 13% by 2030. All of the majors, not just ExxonMobil, are expected to expand their output. Far from mothballing all their gas fields and gushers, the industry is investing in upstream projects from Texan shale to high-tech deep-water wells. Oil companies, directly and through trade groups, lobby against measures that would limit emissions. The trouble is that, according to an assessment by the IPCC, an intergovernmental climate-science body, oil and gas production needs to *fall* by about 20% by 2030 and by about 55% by 2050, in order to stop the Earth's temperature rising by more than 1.5 degrees C above its pre-industrial level.

It would be wrong to conclude that the energy firms must therefore be evil. They are responding to incentives set by society [actually, set by the capitalist economic system, itself]. The financial returns from oil are higher than those from renewables . . . and the typical major derives a minority of its stock market value from profits it will make after 2030. However much the majors are vilified . . . it is not just legal for them to maximize profits, it is also a requirement that shareholders can enforce.

Some hope that the oil companies will gradually head in a new direction, but that looks optimistic. Global investment in renewables, at $300 billion a year, is dwarfed by what is being committed to fossil fuels [trillions].

When and where profits are at stake, one might expect better success in convincing a vampire to change its ways or a leopard to change its spots.

And the relentless pursuit and use of fossil fuels doesn't only threaten the *future* of the earth's environment. Its rapacious extraction is, for the people of the 3rd World, as savage as were the Spanish Conquistadors' search for and theft of their gold and silver. As but one example, John Perkins describes in his 2004 ultimate whistleblower book, *Confessions of an Economic Hit Man*, the devastation of the tiny South American country of Ecuador:

[I]n 1968, Texaco had only just discovered petroleum in Ecuador's Amazon region. A trans-Andean pipeline built shortly after . . . has since leaked over a half million barrels of oil into the fragile rainforest. Today, a new $1.3 billion, three hundred-mile pipeline . . . promises to make Ecuador one of the world's top ten suppliers of oil to the United States. Vast areas of rain forest have fallen, macaws and jaguars have all but vanished, three Ecuadorian indigenous cultures have been driven to the verge of collapse, and pristine rivers have been transformed into flaming cesspools.

In May of 2003, a group of American lawyers representing more than thirty thousand indigenous Ecuadorian people filed a $1 billion lawsuit against ChevronTexaco Corp. The suit asserts that between 1971 and 1992 the oil giant dumped into open holes and rivers over four million gallons per day of toxic wastewater contaminated with oil, heavy metals, and carcinogens, and that the company left behind nearly 350 uncovered waste pits that continue to kill both people and animals.

Ecuador is in far worse shape today [2004] than she was before we introduced her to the miracles of modern economics, banking, and engineering. Since 1970, during this period known euphemistically as the Oil Boom, the official poverty level grew from 50 to 70 percent, under- or unemployment increased from 15 to 70 percent, and public debt increased from $240 million to $16 billion. Unfortunately, Ecuador is not the exception (xvii-xviii).

From a Martin Luther King 1967 speech:

"Again we have deluded ourselves into believing the myth that capitalism grew and prospered out of the Protestant ethic of hard work and sacrifice. The fact is that capitalism was built on the exploitation and suffering of black slaves and continues to thrive on the exploitation of the poor---both black and white [and brown], both here and abroad."

"Overcoming poverty is not a gesture of charity. It is an act of justice."----Nelson Mandela

There are those who are fond of saying that socialism has had its chance and the verdict on it has been rendered. But, in fact, it's the judgment on capitalism for which the condition of the world stands as both testimony and verdict.

It is also often said that the "greatest" U.S. generation was the one that fought WWII. But the truth is that the greatest will be the one that exposes, rejects, and effectively confronts the monster of global capitalism, not only, or even first of all, for the benefit of those of us in the major capitalist citadels, but for the people throughout the world who have most suffered under it, and are most suffering still. This is the task awaiting the US' (and the world's) greatest generation.

BIBLIOGRAPHY

Beckert, Sven. *Empire of Cotton, a Global History*. Vintage Books, 2014

Clark, Ramsey. *The Fire This Time: U.S. War Crimes in the Gulf*. International Action Center, 1992

Cumings, Bruce. *The Korean War: A History*. Modern Library, 2010

Delaisi, Francis. *The Inevitable War*. Small, Maynard & Co. 1911

Galeano, Eduardo. *Open Veins of Latin America*. Monthly Review Press, 1971

Greene, Felix. *Awakened China*. Doubleday & Co. 1961

Greene, Felix. *The Enemy: What Every American Should Know About Imperialism*. Vintage Books, 1970

Harrison, Paul. *Inside the Third World*, 2nd edition. Penguin Books, 1984

Kinzer, Stephen. *The True Flag: Theodore Roosevelt, Mark Twain, and the Birth of American Empire*. Henry Holt & Co. 2017

Nearing, Scott and Freeman, Joseph. *Dollar Diplomacy*. 1925. Reprinted by Modern Reader Paperbacks, 1969

Perkins, John. *Confessions of an Economic Hit Man*. Berrett-Koehler Publishers, 2004

Prins, Nomi. *All the Presidents' Bankers*. Nation Books, 2014

Rodney, Walter. *How Europe Underdeveloped Africa*. Howard University Press, 1982

Shoup, Laurence H. *Wall Street's Think Tank: The Council on Foreign Relations and the Empire of Neoliberal Geopolitics, 1976-2014*. Monthly Review Press, 2015

Spero, Joan E. and Hart, Jeffrey A. *The Politics of International Economic Relations*. St. Martin's Press, Inc. 1997

Steel, Ronald. *Pax Americana: The Cold-War Empire*. The Viking Press, Inc. 1967

Stinnett, *Robert B. Day of Deceit: The Truth about FDR and Pearl Harbor*. Touchstone, 2000

Sublette, Ned and Constance. *The American Slave Coast: A History of the Slave-breeding Industry*. Lawrence Hill Books, 2016

Williams, Eric. *Capitalism & Slavery*. The University of North Carolina Press, 1944